LIVE, LOVE, EAT!

LIVE, LOVE, EAT!

THE BEST OF

Wolfgang Puck

RANDOM HOUSE | NEW YORK

ALL OF THE RECIPES IN THIS WORK HAVE BEEN FEATURED ON
WOLFGANG PUCK'S TELEVISION SHOWS OR ON HIS WEBSITE,
WWW.WOLFGANGPUCK.COM.

LIBRARY OF CONGRESS CATALOGING-IN-PUBLICATION DATA

PUCK, WOLFGANG.
LIVE, LOVE, EAT!: THE BEST OF WOLFGANG PUCK / WOLFGANG PUCK.
P.   CM.
INCLUDES INDEX.
ISBN 0-375-50891-0
1. COOKERY.   I. TITLE.
TX714 .P8324 2002
641.5—DC21   2002024870

PRINTED IN THE UNITED STATES OF AMERICA ON ACID-FREE PAPER
RANDOM HOUSE WEBSITE ADDRESS: WWW.RANDOMHOUSE.COM

2 4 6 8 9 7 5 3

FIRST EDITION

Book design by Barbara M. Bachman

FOR MY MOTHER, MARIA PUCK,

WHO HAS ALWAYS BEEN MY INSPIRATION.

AND ESPECIALLY FOR BARBARA LAZAROFF,

MY WIFE AND PARTNER,

AND OUR SONS, CAMERON AND BYRON.

YOU ARE THE GREATEST PASSIONS IN MY LIFE.

ACKNOWLEDGMENTS

I extend my sincere thanks to all the people who helped make this book possible, including:

My partner Tom Kaplan, who helps me on the business side so that I can play in the kitchen.

And my partners in the kitchen: Lee Hefter, David Robbins, Jennifer Naylor, François Kwak-Dongo, Mitch and Steve Rosenthal, Matt Bencivenga, Sherry Yard, Mark Ferguson, Joseph Bennett, John LaGrone, Luis Diaz, Rene Mata, Aram Mardigian, Robin Stotter, Alan Skversky, and all the other talented chefs, sous chefs, and cooks with whom I have the pleasure of working every day.

Rob Kautz, CEO of Wolfgang Puck Worldwide.

All my dedicated and talented managers and partners, including Bella Lantsman, Klaus Puck, Tracy Spillane, Amanda Larsen-Puck, Joe Essa, Clint Westbrook, and Karl Schuster.

Karl Matz and Cecilia de Castro, who led the efforts to test and record the recipes.

Matthew Klein, for his photographs of the finished recipes and their step-by-step preparations; food stylists Helen Jones and Valerie Aikman-Smith, who assisted on the food photography; Yoshiharu Koizumi, for behind-the-scenes photographs of my restaurants; and Steven Rothfeld, who took the jacket photograph.

Rob Bleifer from the Food Network, for assisting with and styling the food for my TV show.

John Doig and John Long for their initial development work on my WolfgangPuck.com website.

Everyone at Random House, especially Mary Bahr, my editor, for her intelligence and enthusiasm.

Everyone at Wolfgang Puck Worldwide, Inc., including Jason Budow, who designed the jacket for this book; Norman Kolpas, who oversaw this project; and my communications director and longtime colleague, Jannis Swerman.

Maggie Boone, who keeps me organized on a daily basis.

CONTENTS

ACKNOWLEDGMENTS IX

INTRODUCTION XV

A NOTE ON RECIPE INSTRUCTIONS
AND COOKING TIMES XVII

WINE SUGGESTIONS XIX

APPETIZERS | 3

California Guacamole 4

Wolfgang's Vegetable Spring Rolls 5

**Potstickers with Pork and Dried Fruit
Filling** 8

**Black-and-Green-Olive Tapenade with
Goat Cheese Crostini** 11

Herbed Goat Cheese 12

Spicy Tomato-and-Basil Bruschetta 13

Hot Spinach-Artichoke Dip 14

Chicken-and-Vegetable Quesadillas 16

**Yellow Finnish Potatoes with Crème
Fraîche and Osetra Caviar** 18

**Crab Cakes with Sweet Red Bell Pepper
Sauce** 19

Tuna Tartare 21

SOUPS | 23

**Hearty Potato-and-Cheddar Soup
with Bacon** 24

Chino Farm Carrot-and-Ginger Soup 26

My Mother's Garden Vegetable Soup 27

Chicken Pot Pie Soup 28

Tortilla Soup 30

**Corn Chowder with Littleneck Clams and
Jalapeño Cream** 32

Classic French Onion Soup 34

SALADS | 37

**Goat Cheese Salad with Arugula
and Radicchio** 38

Greek Shrimp Salad 40

Chinois Chicken Salad 42

Chino Chopped-Vegetable Salad 44

Insalata Pantesca 46

Spago Cucumber Salad 47

All-American Potato Salad 48

PIZZA AND PASTA | 51

Spicy Chicken Pizza 52

Pizza with Smoked Salmon and Caviar 54

Four Seasons Pizza 55

Calzone with Artichoke Hearts and
   Porcini Mushrooms 57

Fettuccine Wolf-fredo with Grilled
   Chicken 59

Pasta Puttanesca 62

My Favorite Tomato Sauce 63

Angel Hair with Tomato Sauce 64

Hearty Beef Bolognese 65

Classic Beef Lasagne 67

My Special Spaghetti and Meatballs 69

Bucatini with Mussels, Clams,
   and Oven-Dried Tomatoes 71

Pumpkin Ravioli 73

White Corn Agnolotti 75

Wild Mushroom Risotto 78

SEAFOOD | 81

Spicy Shrimp Tempura with Cilantro 82

Crispy Shrimp with Chinese Noodles and
   Spicy Garlic Sauce 84

Grilled Shrimp with Ginger and Lime 86

Lobster with Sweet Ginger 87

Lobster Imperial in Black Bean Sauce 90

Seared Tuna au Poivre 92

Acqua Pazza with Sea Bass, Clams,
   and Mussels 94

Pan-Seared Sea Bass with Cannellini
   Beans, Braised Escarole, and Cherry
   Tomato Vinaigrette 96

Sea Bass with Lemon and
   Caper Sauce 99

Roasted Black Bass on Jasmine Rice with
   Miso Glaze 101

Marinated and Glazed Swordfish 102

POULTRY | 105

Pan-Roasted Chicken Breasts Stuffed with
   Bell Peppers with Sweet Green Onion
   Sauce 106

Grilled Chicken Breasts with Garlic
   and Parsley 108

Grilled Italian Chicken with Summer
   Squash 110

Grilled Chicken Kebabs with Lemon
   and Thyme 112

Barbecued Butterflied Chicken with
   Orange-Sherry Marinade 114

My Mother's Chicken-Stuffed Bell
   Peppers with Tomato Sauce 116

All-American Chicken Pot Pie 118

Wiener Backhendl 121

Turkey Mushroom Burgers with

    Chunky Tomato Salsa Compote 122

MEAT | 125

Wolfgang's Bacon-Wrapped

    Meat Loaf 126

Spicy Asian Beef Burgers with Shiitake

    Mushrooms 128

New York Steaks with Four Peppercorns

    and Port Wine Sauce 130

Beef Stew with Winter Vegetables and

    Red Wine 132

My Beef Goulash 134

Roasted Beef Tenderloin with Smoky

    Tomato-Chili Salsa 136

Wiener Schnitzel with Warm

    Potato Salad 138

Minced Veal or Pork with Chanterelles,

    Paprika Cream Sauce, and Noodles 141

Rack of Pork with Caramelized Maple

    Onions 143

Fresh Sweet Italian Fennel Sausage 145

Catalonian Fire-Roasted Rack of Lamb 147

Chinois Grilled Lamb Chops with

    Cilantro-Mint Vinaigrette 150

ACCOMPANIMENTS | 153

Stir-Fried Vegetables 154

Dry-Fried String Beans 156

Zucchini with Basil and Tomatoes 157

Austrian White Asparagus with Browned

    Bread Crumbs 158

Fried Spinach Leaves 159

Creamy Mashed Potatoes with

    Caramelized Onions 160

Roasted-Garlic Mashed Potatoes 162

Potato Galette with Goat Cheese 163

Braised Sweet-and-Sour Cabbage 164

Spaetzle 165

Braised Chestnuts 167

Stir-Fried Wild Rice with Apples

    and Sun-Dried Cherries 169

Buttermilk Biscuits with Parmesan

    and Onion 170

Focaccia 172

DESSERTS | 175

Wolfgang's Tarte Tatin 176

Baked Apple Pouches with Cinnamon

    and Raisins 178

Decadent Warm Chocolate Cupcakes

    with Molten Centers 179

My Favorite Chocolate Cake 181

Chocolate Shortbread Footballs 183

Raspberries in Puff Pastry 185

Caramelized Lemon-Lime Torte 187

Cookies-and-Cream Cheesecake 189

Classic Spago Cheesecake 192

Kaiserschmarren 194

Salzburger Nockerln with

    Fresh Raspberry Jam 196

White Chocolate Malt Ice Cream 198

Almond Granita 199

Melon Granita 201

BASICS | 203

Chicken Stock 204

Brown Chicken Stock 205

Fish Stock 206

Brown Veal Stock 207

Court Bouillon 208

Basic Pasta Dough 209

Pizza Dough 211

Puff Pastry 213

Sugar Dough 216

Peeled and Seeded Tomatoes and Tomato Concassé 217

Oven-Dried Tomatoes 218

Roasted Whole Garlic 219

Double-Blanched Garlic 220

Toasting Nuts 221

Toasting and Grinding Whole Spices 222

Making a Bouquet Garni 223

Basil Oil 224

Chili and Garlic Oil 225

Dill Cream 226

Basil-Garlic Vinaigrette 227

Greek Salad Dressing 228

Cutting Julienne and Chiffonade 229

Pitting an Avocado 230

Pitting Olives 231

Preparing Artichoke Hearts 232

Shelling and Deveining Shrimp 233

INDEX | 235

"Live, love, eat!" has been my personal motto for almost as long as I've been cooking professionally. These three simple words sum up my belief that a well-rounded, happy life full of achievements is one that you live with passion, whether you're pursuing romance or raising a family or cooking food and sharing it with friends.

This book reflects my own passionate approach to living, cooking, and eating. You'll find that I use the word "love" a lot in my introductions to the recipes, all of which are favorites that I've drawn from my restaurants, my Food Network television show, or my WolfgangPuck.com website. These are recipes for dishes that I really do feel passionate about. They are fun to cook and even more fun to serve to people you love.

Throughout the book, I've included lots of color photographs of the finished dishes, action shots that demonstrate key steps in their preparation, and behind-the-scenes photos from my restaurants. I hope these pictures will make you feel like I'm there with you in the kitchen, sharing my knowledge and passion with you and, most importantly, encouraging you to make these recipes your own.

Have fun while you're cooking from this book. Sharing good food with friends and family will make everybody a happier person.

"Live, love, eat!"

I don't know many chefs who rely on clocks, timers, dials, and thermometers to tell them when recipes are done.

One of the most basic parts of any professional cook's training is to use your eyes, nose, mouth, ears, and fingers to tell when something is cooked just right. That is why, in every recipe in this book, for every stage of its preparation, I try to share with you my own guidelines for how the food you're cooking should look, smell, taste, sound, or feel. As I like to tell people, you should form a relationship with your ingredients.

Not that there's anything wrong with setting a timer. Many people cook that way at home, and it's a good approach if it helps them get a delicious meal on the table easily and with less anxiety. For those who feel like they need to check the clock, I've included approximate times to go along with the sensory cues in each recipe.

Please remember, though, that cooking times can only ever be approximate. The specific ingredients, cookware, and appliances you use will all have an effect on how long any cooking process actually takes.

As you use the recipes in this book, I hope you'll pay special attention to the instructions that call for you to use your senses. By doing so, you will gradually become a better, more secure cook who has a lot more fun in the kitchen.

I have to admit something important to you: Sometimes, I think my favorite motto should be changed to read, "Live, love, eat . . . and drink!"

Why? Because good food and wine are inseparable. When they are matched up thoughtfully in a meal, each makes the enjoyment of the other much more pleasurable.

Experts on pairing food and wine have written volumes and volumes on how to choose a wine that goes best with a particular dish, or how to prepare and alter a recipe in such a way that it best complements a particular wine. I often have the chance to do exactly that when I'm cooking at Spago or one of my other restaurants.

But for the kind of everyday good cooking that I emphasize in this book, I would like to propose to you a simpler approach to selecting wines. And, while I'm going to give you more details below, I can sum up that approach in a single sentence:

Choose a wine you like to drink, and enjoy it.

Of course, a little advice and some advance planning can help you make that choice and add to your enjoyment. And you should always keep in mind the flavors of the food you are cooking and try to complement them with the flavors of the wine you pour. Please follow these few simple guidelines, which I've organized to correspond to the chapters in this book:

LIGHT APPETIZERS AND SOUPS

- Sparkling wine, whether French Champagne, a California sparkler, or an Italian Asti or Prosecco.
- Light, crisp, dry whites such as Chablis, Sauvignon Blanc, Fumé Blanc, Viognier, or Soave.

- Light, fruity whites such as Riesling, Chenin Blanc, Muscat, and Gewürztraminer.
- Light reds such as Beaujolais, Pinot Noir, Chianti, or Valpolicella.

SALADS

- Crisp, acidic young whites such as Sauvignon Blanc, Chenin Blanc, Riesling, Grüner Veltliner, Muscadet, or light Chardonnay.
- Light dry or slightly sweet rosés.
- For composed salads, light, dry, or slightly sweet Champagne or sparkling wine.

LIGHTER PIZZAS AND PASTAS
FEATURING CHEESE OR SEAFOOD

- Light or medium-bodied dry whites such as Colombard, Pouilly-Fumé, Graves, Sauvignon Blanc, Fumé Blanc, or Soave.
- Medium- or full-bodied dry whites such as Pinot Gris, Tokay, or Pouilly-Fuissé.
- For my Pizza with Smoked Salmon and Caviar (page 54), Champagne or other sparkling wine.

EARTHY PIZZAS OR PASTAS
FEATURING MUSHROOMS OR MEATS

- Light or medium-bodied dry reds such as Valpolicella, Beaujolais, Chianti, Côtes du Rhône, Pinot Noir, Merlot, Zinfandel, Nebbiolo, or Barbaresco.
- More robust rosés.

SEAFOOD

- Light or medium-bodied dry whites such as Muscadet, Sancerre, Chablis, Sauvignon Blanc, Fumé Blanc, and Soave.

- Light or medium-bodied fruity, slightly sweet whites such as Riesling, Chenin Blanc, Vouvray, and Gewürztraminer.
- Medium- or full-bodied dry whites such as Verdicchio, Orvieto, Frascati, Pinot Gris, Pinot Blanc, Mâcon-Villages, Chardonnay, Viognier, and, naturally, white Burgundies.
- Light or medium-bodied rosés such as White Zinfandel, Anjou, or Bandol.
- With rich, meaty fish like salmon or tuna, or with seafood prepared with black pepper, almonds, mushrooms, or potato puree, light or medium-bodied dry reds such as Valpolicella, Chianti, Dolcetto, Barbaresco, or Pinot Noir.

POULTRY

- Light or medium-bodied dry whites such as Sancerre, Chablis, Graves, Sauvignon Blanc, or Fumé Blanc.
- Light or medium-bodied slightly sweet whites such as Riesling, Chenin Blanc, Pinot Gris, and Gewürztraminer.
- Medium- or full-bodied dry whites such as Pinot Blanc, Semillon, Chardonnay, Viognier, Côtes du Rhône, and white Burgundy.
- Light or medium-bodied dry reds such as Bardolino, Beaujolais, Chianti, Dolcetto, Côtes du Rhône, or Rioja.
- Medium- or full-bodied dry reds such as Chianti Classico, Pinot Noir, Merlot, Rioja Reserva, Beaune, Médoc, Zinfandel, and lighter Cabernet Sauvignons.
- Light or medium-bodied rosés such as White Zinfandel, Anjou, or Bandol.
- Sparkling wine or Champagne.

PORK OR VEAL

- Light or medium-bodied dry white such as Sancerre, Pouilly-Fumé, Chablis, Graves, Sauvignon Blanc, or Fumé Blanc.
- Light or medium-bodied slightly sweet whites such as Riesling, Chenin Blanc, Gewürztraminer, Muscat, or Vouvray.
- Medium- or full-bodied dry whites such as Pinot Gris, Pinot Blanc, Semillon, Chardonnay, Viognier, and white Burgundy.

- Light or medium-bodied dry reds such as Bardolino, Beaujolais, Chianti, Dolcetto, Côtes du Rhône, or Barbera.
- Medium-bodied dry reds such as Rioja, Pinot Noir, Barbaresco, Zinfandel, or Châteauneuf-du-Pape, as well as Meritage blends and lighter and younger Bordeaux.
- Light or medium-bodied rosés such as White Zinfandel, Grenache, Anjou, Tavel, or Bandol.

LAMB

- Light or medium-bodied dry reds such as Côtes du Rhône or Rioja.
- Medium- or full-bodied dry reds such as Pinot Noir, Merlot, Rioja, Beaune, Zinfandel, or Châteauneuf-du-Pape.
- Or pull out all the stops with a great Bordeaux.

BEEF

- Any medium- or full-bodied red wine such as Côtes du Rhône, Bordeaux, Cabernet Sauvignon, Merlot, Zinfandel, Spanish reds, or Meritage blends.

DESSERTS

- For desserts with fruits, nuts, caramels, custards, and other light or nonassertive flavors, Sauternes, Trockenbeerenauslese, Tokay, Vin Santo, late-harvest Riesling, or other medium- or full-bodied sweet white wines. (Never serve these with chocolate.)
- For chocolate desserts, Port or even a good Cabernet Sauvignon.

LIVE, LOVE, EAT!

California Guacamole

Wolfgang's Vegetable Spring Rolls

Potstickers with Pork and Dried Fruit Filling

Black-and-Green-Olive Tapenade with Goat Cheese Crostini

Herbed Goat Cheese

Spicy Tomato-and-Basil Bruschetta

Hot Spinach-Artichoke Dip

Chicken-and-Vegetable Quesadillas

Yellow Finnish Potatoes with Crème Fraîche and Osetra Caviar

Crab Cakes with Sweet Red Bell Pepper Sauce

Tuna Tartare

California Guacamole

*T*here are as many different guacamole recipes as there are cantinas in Mexico. I like to give my version extra, subtle flavor by adding roasted garlic and chopped shallot. Keep the mashing of the fresh ingredients to a minimum to give each a better chance to express itself. Use pebble-skinned Hass avocados, which have the best flavor; when fully ripe, they give to gentle fingertip pressure. Serve with your favorite crisp corn tortilla chips for dipping.

3 medium, fully ripe avocados

1/4 cup freshly squeezed lime juice

1/3 cup freshly chopped cilantro

1 medium shallot, minced

1 tablespoon Roasted Whole Garlic
  (page 219)

1 small jalapeño chili, seeded and
  minced

1 teaspoon salt

Corn tortilla chips

1. Halve each avocado, remove its pit (page 230), and scoop the flesh into a mixing bowl. Pour the lime juice over the avocado.

2. Using a fork or potato masher, lightly mash the avocado, leaving it slightly chunky. Stir in the cilantro, shallot, Roasted Whole Garlic, jalapeño, and salt. (The guacamole can be made ahead to this point, covered with plastic wrap, and kept refrigerated for up to 8 hours. Return to room temperature before serving.)

3. Serve with tortilla chips.

Wolfgang's Vegetable Spring Rolls

I think you'll find these crisp, fresh-tasting appetizers a lot of fun to put together. And they're surprisingly easy to make, so don't be put off by the long list of ingredients and instructions. Most good-sized supermarkets today will have all the special ingredients you need in their Asian or imported-foods aisle, and the wonton wrappers in their refrigerated case; or look in an Asian market.

Transparent glass noodles made from mung bean flour need no boiling, just soaking in cold water; they are also called bean threads or cellophane noodles.

CHINESE HOT MUSTARD SAUCE

1/4 cup brine from bottled pickled
    ginger

2 tablespoons Chinese dry mustard
    or Colman's English Mustard
    Powder

2 tablespoons rice wine vinegar

1 tablespoon sugar

1 tablespoon chili oil

1 tablespoon Asian toasted sesame
    oil

2 teaspoons water

Juice of 1 lemon

Pinch of turmeric

1 cup peanut oil

AROMATICS

2 tablespoons coarsely chopped fresh
    ginger

2 tablespoons coarsely chopped
    green onion

1 tablespoon chopped garlic

Pinch of red pepper flakes

1/2 cup peanut oil

Pinch of salt

Pinch of freshly ground black pepper

Pinch of sugar

FILLING

3 tablespoons peanut oil

4 ounces fresh shiitake mushrooms,
    stems discarded, caps cut into thin
    julienne strips

2 cups thinly shredded green cabbage
    leaves

1 1/2 cups thinly sliced red bell pepper

1/2 cup thinly sliced onion

1 medium carrot, shredded

Salt

Freshly ground black pepper

4 ounces glass (cellophane or bean
    thread) noodles, soaked in water
    for 10 minutes, drained well, and
    cut into 3- to 4-inch strands

1/2 cup chopped cilantro

1/4 cup mushroom soy sauce

2 tablespoons Asian chili paste

1 tablespoon Asian toasted sesame
    oil

TO FORM SPRING ROLLS

1 egg

1 tablespoon cold water

1 tablespoon cornstarch

1 package wonton wrappers

Peanut oil, for deep-frying

1. Up to 1 week ahead, prepare the Chinese Hot Mustard Sauce: In a nonreactive bowl, combine all the ingredients except the peanut oil. Stir with a wire whisk until well blended. Whisking continuously, slowly pour in the peanut oil until emulsified. Cover with plastic wrap and refrigerate until needed, letting the mixture come to room temperature before serving.

2. To prepare the aromatic mixture: In the bowl of a food processor fitted with the metal blade, put the ginger, green onion, garlic, and red pepper flakes. With the machine running, slowly pour the oil through the feed tube and continue processing until the solids are finely pureed. Transfer the mixture to a small saucepan or skillet and cook over medium heat, stirring with a wooden spoon, until its aroma develops, 1 to 2 minutes. Stir in the salt, pepper, and sugar. Set aside.

3. To prepare the filling: Heat a wok or heavy skillet over medium-high heat. Drizzle in the peanut oil. Add the shiitake mushrooms and stir-fry for 30 seconds, then add the remaining vegetables and stir-fry for 1 minute more. Drain off excess liquid and transfer the vegetables to a mixing bowl. Season to taste with salt and pepper. Stir in the noodles, cilantro, mushroom soy sauce, chili paste, and sesame oil. Stir in the reserved aromatic mixture. Adjust the seasonings to taste with a little more salt and pepper. Set aside to cool com-

pletely to room temperature. When ready to form the spring rolls, use your hands to squeeze out all the excess liquid, transferring the mixture to another bowl as you do.

4. To assemble the spring rolls: First prepare an egg wash in a small bowl by lightly beating together the egg, water, and cornstarch with a fork or small whisk until the cornstarch dissolves. Place 1 wonton wrapper on a work surface with a corner facing you. Place about ¼ cup of prepared filling just below the center of the wrapper. Fold the bottom corner away from you, over the filling. Dip a finger or pastry brush in the egg wash and paint it lightly  around the wrapper's exposed edges. Keeping the wrapper tight and compact around the filling, continue to roll up the spring roll; tuck in the left and right corners over the filled portion and complete the rolling to make a neat parcel. Set the spring roll aside and repeat with the remaining wrappers and filling.

5. In a heavy, deep saucepan or deep-fryer, heat the peanut oil to 350°F on a deep-frying thermometer. Working in batches of 3 or 4 at a time, deep-fry the spring rolls until golden, 2 to 3 minutes, turning them with a slotted metal or wire spoon so they cook evenly. Transfer to paper towels to drain.

6. If you'd like to make the spring rolls stand up for an attractive presentation, carefully trim off their ends with a sharp knife. Cut each spring roll diagonally in half. Serve with Chinese Hot Mustard Sauce for dipping, drizzling it onto the serving plate and over the spring rolls if you like. Serve immediately.

Potstickers with Pork and Dried Fruit Filling

I love the hustle and bustle of eating a meal of dim sum in a big Chinese restaurant. So many choices, all just a bite or two, each promising a different, exciting taste. These particular little dumplings, favorites of mine, can be steamed if you like. But I prefer them prepared as potstickers, a descriptive name that refers to the crisp brown surface they develop on one side when cooked by a combination of boiling or steaming and sautéing. To keep the dumplings from actually sticking during browning, use a nonstick skillet. The quantities here yield a generous amount, perfect for an Asian-themed cocktail party; but you can cut the measurements by half or three quarters for a smaller gathering. Assembly takes some time, but you can prepare the filling and shape the dumplings up to a day ahead of cooking.

FILLING

1/4 cup peeled and coarsely chopped
   garlic cloves

1 inch fresh ginger

2 tablespoons peanut oil

1 1/2 pounds lean ground pork

1/2 cup finely chopped cilantro leaves

1/2 cup finely chopped green onions

1/4 cup finely chopped dried fruits
   (apricots, cherries, or raisins)

1/4 cup oyster sauce

1 tablespoon Asian chili paste

1 tablespoon Asian toasted sesame
   oil

Salt

Freshly ground black pepper

Pinch of sugar

Circular wonton wrappers

1 egg

1 tablespoon cold water

2 to 4 tablespoons peanut oil

DIPPING SAUCE

1/2 cup rice wine vinegar

2 tablespoons sesame oil

2 tablespoons minced scallions or
green onions

Large pinch of sugar

1. To prepare the filling: In a blender or the bowl of a food processor fitted with the metal blade, put the garlic and ginger. With the machine running, slowly pour in the oil until the solids are finely pureed. Transfer to a mixing bowl. Add the remaining filling ingredients and, with a sturdy wooden spoon, stir together until thoroughly mixed. Cover with plastic wrap and refrigerate until thoroughly chilled, at least 1 hour.

2. To assemble the potstickers: Separate the wonton wrappers. In a small bowl, beat the egg and water together with a fork or small whisk to make an egg wash. With your fingertip or a small pastry brush, lightly brush the perimeter of a wrapper with the egg wash. Place a tablespoonful of the filling in the center of the wrapper. Fold the wrapper in half to enclose the filling. Starting at the center of the semicircle where the edges meet, seal the potsticker by pressing together and folding the edges into small pleats, first all the way to one end and then to the other. Transfer to a waxed-paper-lined tray. Repeat with the remaining wrappers and filling. Cover with plastic wrap and refrigerate until ready to cook.

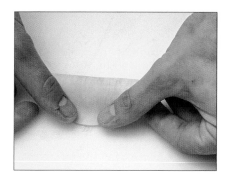

3. To cook the potstickers: Bring a large pan of lightly salted water to a boil. Carefully drop in 10 to 12 dumplings and stir gently to prevent them from sticking together; when the water returns to a boil, cook them for about 7 minutes. Remove with a slotted spoon or wire skimmer and drain well. Repeat with remaining batches.

4. To brown the dumplings: Heat a large nonstick skillet over medium-high heat and pour in

enough peanut oil to coat the bottom. Add a single layer of dumplings, pleated sides up, and fry until their undersides are golden, 2 to 3 minutes. Repeat with remaining dumplings. While the dumplings are cooking, stir together the Dipping Sauce ingredients in a mixing bowl and pass it along with the dumplings.

Black-and-Green-Olive Tapenade
with Goat Cheese Crostini

MAKES 1 GENEROUS CUP TAPENADE, ENOUGH FOR ABOUT 16 CROSTINI

*T*apenade, the classic olive spread of **Provence**, gains extra dimensions of flavor and color by including not only green olives with the traditional black ones but also oven-dried tomatoes. Combined with a luxurious smear of rich, creamy goat cheese, the spread makes a perfect, quick topping for crostini, thin cousins to the Italian appetizer toast known as bruschetta (page 13). If you like, substitute the **Herbed Goat Cheese** recipe that follows for the plain goat cheese.

FOR THE TAPENADE

1 cup black **Niçoise**-style olives, pitted (page 231)

1 cup small green French olives such as **Picholines**, pitted (page 231)

1/4 cup **Oven-Dried Tomatoes** (page 218), drained

1 tablespoon capers

1 garlic clove, peeled

1 anchovy fillet

1/2 tablespoon chopped fresh basil leaves

1/2 tablespoon chopped fresh thyme leaves

1/2 tablespoon chopped fresh flat-leaf parsley

1/4 tablespoon chopped fresh oregano leaves

1/4 cup extra-virgin olive oil

FOR THE CROSTINI

16 thin diagonal slices crusty French or Italian bread

8 ounces fresh creamy goat cheese

1. To prepare the tapenade: In a food processor fitted with the metal blade, combine all the ingredients except the olive oil. Pulse the machine on and off until the mixture is coarsely chopped but well blended. While continuing to pulse, slowly pour in the olive oil through the feed tube. Transfer to a bowl, cover with plastic wrap, and refrigerate until ready to use. (The tapenade will keep for up to 1 month.)

2. Preheat the oven to 400°F. Arrange the bread slices in a single layer on a baking sheet and bake until lightly golden, about 5 minutes.

3. Spread each of the crostini with about 1 tablespoon of the goat cheese. Spread a generous tablespoon of tapenade on top. Serve immediately.

Herbed Goat Cheese

*P*repared in minutes, **Herbed Goat Cheese** makes a delicious hors d'oeuvre spread for crackers, toasts, or crusts of bread. Leave it covered in the refrigerator for a while and the cheese will pick up even more of the herbs' flavor. If you like certain fresh herbs better than the ones I list here, by all means make up your own seasoning combination. The cheese is also a perfect topping for pizza or pasta.

2 teaspoons chopped fresh flat-leaf parsley

2 teaspoons chopped fresh chives

1 teaspoon chopped fresh thyme leaves

1/2 teaspoon freshly ground black pepper

One 7- to 8-ounce log creamy goat cheese

1. On a flat plate, stir together the parsley, chives, thyme, and pepper, then spread them out evenly.

2. Gently but firmly roll the log of cheese in the mixture until it is evenly coated with the herbs, making sure to retain the log shape. Wrap in plastic wrap and refrigerate until needed.

Spicy Tomato-and-Basil Bruschetta

*I*n autumn in Tuscany, when the first olives have been pressed to make oil, locals toast thick slices of rustic bread over a wood fire, rub it with garlic, and then drizzle it with the fragrant new oil to form a base for all kinds of toppings, from plump white beans to boiled bitter greens. My favorite topping for these toasts known as bruschetta is one favored in **Rome**: fresh tomatoes and basil, a combination I enhance with sweet **Oven-Dried Tomatoes**, spicy red pepper flakes, and mellow roasted garlic.

4 ripe tomatoes, cored and cut into
$1/2$-inch dice

$1/2$ cup coarsely chopped **Oven-Dried Tomatoes** (page 218)

$1/2$ cup julienned fresh basil leaves

$1/2$ teaspoon salt

$1/4$ teaspoon freshly ground black pepper

$1/4$ teaspoon dried red pepper flakes

12 slices country-style Italian bread, each $3/4$ to 1 inch thick

3 tablespoons extra-virgin olive oil

1 tablespoon **Roasted Whole Garlic** (page 219)

1. Preheat the broiler or a grill.
2. In a medium bowl, combine the fresh and Oven-Dried Tomatoes. Add about ⅓ cup of the basil along with the salt and black and red peppers. Toss well and set aside.
3. Broil or grill the bread until golden brown on both sides, 1 to 2 minutes per side. Transfer the toasts to a serving dish or platter. In a small bowl, stir and mash together the olive oil and Roasted Whole Garlic. Brush it over the top of each piece of bread.
4. Using a slotted spoon to drain off excess liquid, divide the tomato mixture evenly among the bread slices. Garnish with the remaining basil and serve immediately.

Hot Spinach-Artichoke Dip

*I*n this elegant-yet-easy party dip, spinach and artichoke hearts blend together with Parmesan; tangy goat cheese; the thick and slightly soured Italian-style cream cheese known as mascarpone; and the French soured cream known as crème fraiche. All you need to add is hot, crusty French bread or your favorite chips or crackers. To make preparation even easier, look for commercial bags of baby spinach leaves, which need no washing or stemming; one 10-ounce bag is the equivalent of a 1-pound bunch of spinach with its stems.

3 bunches of spinach, thoroughly washed and stemmed	2 tablespoons goat cheese
1 package frozen artichoke hearts, 10 ounces, thawed and drained	2 tablespoons Roasted Whole Garlic (page 219)
1 cup mayonnaise	1 tablespoon lemon juice
1/3 cup mascarpone cheese	1 teaspoon salt
1/3 cup crème fraîche	1/4 teaspoon black pepper
1/2 cup freshly grated Parmesan cheese	2 tablespoons bread crumbs
	1/4 teaspoon paprika

1. Bring a large pot of water to a boil. On the counter near the pot, place a large mixing bowl filled with ice and water. Put a third of the spinach in a large metal sieve and submerge it in the boiling water for about 1 minute. Transfer the spinach in the sieve to the bowl of iced water and leave to cool for 30 seconds. Remove the sieve from the water and, with the back of a large metal or wooden spoon, press firmly down on the spinach to squeeze out as much water as possible. Set aside in another mixing bowl. Repeat with the remaining spinach.

2. Preheat the oven to 375°F. Put the artichoke hearts in the bowl of a food processor fitted with the metal blade. Pulse the machine until the artichoke hearts are very coarsely chopped, 5 to 7 seconds. Add the mayonnaise, mascarpone cheese, crème fraîche, ¼ cup of the

Parmesan cheese, the goat cheese, Roasted Whole Garlic, lemon juice, salt, and pepper. Process just until combined, about 5 seconds more.

3. Add the reserved blanched spinach to the processor and pulse the machine a few times more, just until it is thoroughly blended with the other ingredients. The dip should still have some texture. Spoon into a shallow 3- to 4-cup baking dish.

4. In small bowl, toss together the remaining Parmesan with the bread crumbs and paprika; evenly sprinkle the mixture over the dip. Bake in the preheated oven until the dip is heated through and its topping is golden brown, 15 to 20 minutes. Serve hot with crusty bread or crackers for dipping.

Chicken-and-Vegetable Quesadillas

•• A whole fiesta of popular Southwestern flavors comes together in this version of a favorite tortilla-based snack. Roasting the tomatoes and peppers gives the chunky salsa a rich, smoky flavor. Pass quesadilla wedges as an hors d'oeuvre or serve individual quesadillas as a casual main dish. California Guacamole (page 4) goes very well with them. Be sure to allow yourself plenty of time to prepare the marinated chicken and the salsa before the final easy assembly and cooking of the quesadillas.

Extra-virgin olive oil, for brushing

2 boneless, skinless chicken breast
    halves

Salt

Freshly ground black pepper

MARINADE

1/3 cup extra-virgin olive oil

3 tablespoons lime juice

1 tablespoon finely chopped jalapeño
    chili

1 tablespoon chopped fresh cilantro

1/2 teaspoon salt

ROASTED TOMATO AND PEPPER SALSA

4 Roma tomatoes

1 large red bell pepper

1 poblano chili

2 tablespoons chopped fresh cilantro

2 tablespoons chopped scallion

1 tablespoon extra-virgin olive oil

Salt

Freshly ground black pepper

Olive oil, for frying

8 large flour tortillas, 8 to 9 inches in
    diameter

2 cups shredded Monterey Jack
    cheese

Sour cream

Cilantro sprigs for garnish

1. Preheat a grill or broiler. Brush the chicken breasts with olive oil, season with salt and pepper, and grill or broil them until they are cooked through, 5 to 7 minutes per side. Let the chicken breasts rest for a few minutes. With a sharp knife, cut them crosswise into thin strips.

2. To make the marinade: In a glass bowl, stir together the olive oil, lime juice, jalapeño, cilantro, and salt. Add the chicken strips, toss to coat thoroughly, and cover with plastic wrap. Refrigerate for about 1 hour.

3. To make the salsa: Working with 1 Roma tomato at a time, spear the tomato on a long-handled carving fork. Turn a burner on a gas stovetop to high heat and hold the tomato over the open flame, turning constantly, until the skin blackens and begins to peel away from the tomato. Transfer the tomato to a plate and repeat with the remaining tomatoes and the bell pepper and poblano chili. (If you don't have a gas stove, put the tomatoes on a broiler tray beneath a preheated broiler and turn them several times until they're evenly blackened. Set them aside and do the same for the bell pepper and then the chili.)

4. Peel, core, seed, and dice the tomatoes, bell pepper, and chili. (When working with the chili, be careful not to touch your eyes or other sensitive areas, as its oils can cause a burning feeling. Wear kitchen gloves, or wash your hands well afterward.) In a medium mixing bowl, combine the diced tomato, bell pepper, and chili with the cilantro, scallion, and olive oil. Season to taste with salt and pepper. Cover with plastic wrap and set aside. Preheat the oven to its lowest setting.

5. With a slotted spoon, remove the chicken from the marinade and transfer to a clean bowl. Discard the excess marinade.

6. To assemble the quesadillas: Heat a large, heavy skillet over medium heat and pour in a thin film of olive oil. Place 1 tortilla in the skillet and evenly sprinkle about ¼ cup of the cheese over its surface. Quickly top evenly with one fourth each of the salsa and the marinated chicken, then top with another ¼ cup cheese and another tortilla. With a metal spatula, press down firmly on the quesadilla in the skillet to help compact and seal in the filling. Cook until the underside is golden brown, 1½ to 2 minutes, reducing the heat slightly if the tortilla is browning too quickly.

7. Carefully slide the quesadilla out onto a large plate, then carefully flip it back into the pan. Continue cooking, pressing down with the spatula, until its other side is golden and the cheese is completely melted, 1½ to 2 minutes more. Slide the quesadilla from the skillet onto a baking sheet and put it in the oven to keep warm. Repeat with the remaining tortillas, cheese, salsa, and chicken.

8. To serve, cut each quesadilla into 4 wedges. Arrange on a heated serving platter or individual plates and top each wedge with a dollop of sour cream and a sprig of cilantro.

Yellow Finnish Potatoes with Crème Fraîche and Osetra Caviar

SERVES 4

■ ■ *An* elegant hors d'oeuvre worthy of an Oscars celebration. Osetra, considered one of the finest true caviars, is expensive, so each guest gets just one potato. If you can't resist serving more, and don't want to break the bank, substitute less costly preserved fish roe such as salmon or the so-called golden caviar from whitefish. For a really stellar occasion, I wrap the potatoes in gold-colored kitchen foil, which you can find in some specialty stores; otherwise, use regular silver-colored aluminum foil.

4 medium yellow Finnish potatoes	Freshly ground black pepper
3/4 cup crème fraîche	4 ounces osetra caviar
Salt	

1. Preheat the oven to 400°F. Wash the potatoes and prick each a few times with a fork. Wrap them in gold foil.

2. Bake the potatoes until they're cooked through and yield when you squeeze them, about 1 hour, taking care to protect your hands with a potholder or oven mitt.

3. Remove the potatoes from the oven. With a small, sharp knife, cut a slit in the top of each one. Peel back the foil slightly from the openings.

4. Spoon the crème fraîche into the center of each potato and season to taste with salt and pepper. Spoon the caviar on top of the crème fraîche. Serve immediately.

Crab Cakes with Sweet Red Bell Pepper Sauce

I ate crab cakes for the first time in Chesapeake Bay. To my dismay, I tasted more potato than crab. I took home a few pounds of fresh lump crabmeat, experimented with it, and finally came up with this recipe. If you can't find fresh crabmeat, you can make this with uncooked shrimp. The Sweet Red Bell Pepper Sauce is also delicious with grilled or sautéed shrimp or fish. Be sure to allow at least an hour for the shaped crab cakes to chill before you cook them.

SWEET RED BELL PEPPER SAUCE

5 tablespoons unsalted butter

1/2 medium red bell pepper, cored, seeded, and diced

1/2 medium red onion, peeled and diced

2 garlic cloves, smashed and peeled

Leaves from 2 sprigs of thyme

1/2 cup dry white wine

1 cup heavy cream

Juice of 1/2 medium lemon

Salt

Freshly ground white pepper

CRAB CAKES

2 tablespoons extra-virgin olive oil

1/2 medium red bell pepper, cored, seeded, and finely diced

1/2 medium yellow bell pepper, cored, seeded, and finely diced

1/2 medium red onion, finely diced

1 cup heavy cream

1/2 teaspoon finely chopped jalapeño chili

2 teaspoons chopped fresh chives

2 teaspoons chopped fresh dill

2 teaspoons chopped fresh flat-leaf parsley

Leaves from 2 sprigs fresh thyme

1/2 teaspoon salt

1/8 teaspoon cayenne pepper

1 extra-large egg, lightly beaten

1 cup fresh bread crumbs

1 cup finely ground almonds

1 1/4 pounds fresh crabmeat, any shell pieces removed

2 tablespoons unsalted butter

2 tablespoons vegetable oil

3 cups mixed greens of your choice, cut or torn into bite-sized pieces

1. First, prepare the Sweet Red Bell Pepper Sauce: In a 10-inch skillet over medium-low heat, melt 3 tablespoons of the butter. Sauté the pepper, onion, garlic, and thyme until the onion is translucent, about 10 minutes. Deglaze with the wine and cook until 3 tablespoons of liquid remain. Pour in the cream and bring to a boil. Scrape the contents of the skillet into a blender and puree until smooth. Strain into a bowl, cover with plastic wrap, and refrigerate.

2. To make the crab cakes: In a 10-inch skillet, heat the olive oil over medium heat. Sauté the diced red and yellow peppers and onion until the onion is translucent and the peppers are tender, 8 to 10 minutes. With a slotted spoon, transfer the peppers and onions to a large bowl. Let cool.

3. To the skillet add the heavy cream and jalapeño and simmer until ½ cup of cream remains. Transfer the cream-jalapeño mixture to a heatproof bowl to cool, and then add it to the peppers and onion. Stir in the chives, dill, parsley, thyme, salt, and cayenne pepper.

4. Stir in the egg and ½ cup each of bread crumbs and almonds. Gently fold in the crabmeat. Do not overmix: the mixture will be lumpy. On a flat plate, stir together the remaining bread crumbs and almonds.

5. With your hands, shape the crab mixture into 12 equal puck-shaped cakes. Dip both sides of each crab cake into the crumb-almond mixture to coat it well. Place the crab cakes on a tray, cover with plastic wrap, and refrigerate for 1 to 3 hours.

6. When ready to serve, preheat the oven to 200°F. In a large skillet, heat the butter and vegetable oil together over medium heat. Place half the crab cakes in the skillet and cook them until golden brown, about 4 minutes per side. Transfer to paper towels to drain, then to a covered baking dish in the oven to keep warm. If necessary, add a little more oil to the skillet, then cook the remaining crab cakes.

7. To complete the sauce, transfer it to a clean saucepan and place it over medium heat; when the sauce is hot, whisk in the remaining 2 tablespoons of butter and the lemon juice and season to taste with salt and pepper. Divide the salad greens among six large plates. Arrange 2 crab cakes on top of the greens. Drizzle the sauce around the greens and on top of the crab cakes. Serve immediately.

Tuna Tartare

SERVES 4

*F*avorite Japanese sushi flavors highlight the fresh, rich flavor of the finest tuna in this simple appetizer from Lee Hefter, executive chef at Spago Beverly Hills. You'll find the tuna variety known as ahi sold fresh off the boat and labeled "sushi grade" in top supermarkets and seafood shops today; buy it the day you plan to serve it and keep it well chilled in your refrigerator until ready to use. The pickled ginger and wasabi are stocked in Japanese markets and in the Asian foods section of well-stocked supermarkets.

4 ounces sushi-grade ahi tuna, finely chopped	1 teaspoon chopped pickled ginger
1 tablespoon chopped green onion	1/2 lime
1 teaspoon toasted sesame seeds	2 tablespoons soy sauce
	1 teaspoon wasabi paste

1. In a mixing bowl, combine the ahi, green onion, sesame seeds, and pickled ginger.
2. Squeeze the lime's juice into a small bowl. Add the soy sauce and wasabi paste and stir until the wasabi dissolves completely.
3. Add the lime-soy-wasabi mixture to the other ingredients and stir until thoroughly combined. Serve immediately with toasted brioche, crackers, potato chips, cucumbers, or any crusty bread.

Hearty Potato-and-Cheddar Soup with Bacon

Chino Farm Carrot-and-Ginger Soup

My Mother's Garden Vegetable Soup

Chicken Pot Pie Soup

Tortilla Soup

Corn Chowder with Littleneck Clams and Jalapeño Cream

Classic French Onion Soup

Hearty Potato-and-Cheddar Soup with Bacon

SERVES 6 TO 8

I like to eat this simple, hearty soup in front of a blazing fireplace on a cold winter day. Add thick slices of warm, crusty French bread and you have a complete, casual meal.

1/4 pound sliced smoked bacon, coarsely chopped

4 tablespoons (1/2 stick) unsalted butter

2 small leeks, trimmed, thoroughly washed, and chopped

1 large onion, peeled and chopped

1 carrot, peeled and chopped

1 garlic clove, peeled and minced

1/2 cup all-purpose flour

6 cups Chicken Stock (page 204) or good-quality canned chicken broth

3 pounds baking potatoes, peeled, cut into 1/2-inch cubes

1 pound sharp Cheddar cheese, shredded

1 cup heavy cream

1/3 teaspoon salt

1/4 teaspoon freshly ground black pepper

1/2 cup thinly sliced scallions or chopped chives, for garnish

1. Put the bacon in a soup pot. Put the pan over medium-high heat and cook the bacon, stirring occasionally, until it renders its fat and is crisp but not overly browned, 3 to 5 minutes. With a slotted spoon, transfer the bacon to paper towels to drain. Carefully pour off all but about 1 tablespoon of the bacon drippings.

2. Add the butter to the pot and melt it over medium heat. Add the leeks, onion, carrot, and garlic and cook, stirring occasionally, until the onion is translucent, about 5 minutes. Sprinkle and stir in the flour until it absorbs the fat and any lumps have disappeared. Stirring continuously to dissolve the flour, gradually pour in the Chicken Stock.

3. Add the potatoes to the pot, raise the heat, and bring the liquid to a boil. Reduce the heat to a simmer and cook, partially covered, until the potatoes are tender, about 15 minutes.

4. Put the cheese in a large mixing bowl. Stirring continuously, ladle in about a quarter of the liquid from the hot soup; continue stirring until the cheese has melted and the mixture is smooth. Stir the cheese mixture into the pot.

5.   Gradually stir in the heavy cream. Season to taste with salt and pepper. Continue to heat the soup until it is thick and almost comes to a boil. Ladle into warmed bowls and garnish with thinly sliced scallions or chives.

Chino Farm Carrot-and-Ginger Soup

*M*y dear friends at Southern California's Chino Farm grow the most incredibly sweet and flavorful carrots in all kinds of shapes, sizes, and colors—orange, yellow, and even white. I take advantage of that selection to make a very aromatic carrot soup, which you can also prepare with just the usual orange carrots you find in your everyday market.

3 pounds assorted orange, yellow, and white carrots	1/2 teaspoon freshly ground white pepper
1/4 cup peanut oil	1/2 teaspoon turmeric
1 tablespoon minced garlic	8 cups Chicken Stock (page 204) or good quality canned chicken broth
1 tablespoon minced fresh ginger	1 cup heavy cream
1 tablespoon minced green onion	1/4 pound (1 stick) unsalted butter
Pinch of red pepper flakes	Oil, for deep-frying
1 tablespoon honey, or to taste	1/2 cup julienned fresh ginger
1 tablespoon salt, or to taste	

1. Peel the carrots and slice them thin. In a large soup pot, heat the oil over medium heat. Add the garlic, minced ginger, green onion, and pepper flakes and sauté, stirring continuously, just until they are aromatic and glossy but have not yet begun to brown, 1 to 2 minutes.

2. Add the carrots, honey, salt, pepper, and turmeric. Sauté for 2 minutes, stirring constantly. Add the stock, raise the heat to high, and bring to a boil. Reduce the heat to a simmer and stir in the cream. Cook, partially covered, until the carrots are completely tender, about 40 minutes.

3. In batches, transfer the soup to a blender or food processor fitted with the metal blade, adding some of the butter with each batch. Taking care to avoid splattering, puree the soup, then pour it through a strainer into a clean pot. Repeat with the remaining batches and butter. Taste the soup and adjust the seasoning with salt, pepper, and honey. Cover the pot and keep the soup warm over low heat.

4. In a deep, heavy skillet or deep-fryer, heat the oil to 300°F on a deep-frying thermometer. Carefully add the ginger julienne and fry it until crisp, 1 to 2 minutes. Remove the ginger with a wire-mesh strainer or slotted spoon and transfer to paper towels to drain.

5. To serve the soup, ladle it into heated bowls. Garnish with the fried ginger.

My Mother's Garden Vegetable Soup

*T*he simple soup my mother makes from the vegetables she grows in her own garden next to the house where I grew up in **St. Viet, Carinthia, Austria**, is very little different from the following traditional French recipe: just lots of good, fresh vegetables and some liquid to cook them in. My mother uses only water, because her vegetables are peak-of-season, just-picked, and therefore full of flavor, but you can use stock if you like. Pistou, the puree of tomatoes, basil, garlic, and olive oil in this recipe, is a traditional French condiment that adds a burst of flavor just before serving.

2 small leeks, white part only,
   thoroughly washed

1 large potato, peeled

1 small onion, peeled

2 stalks celery

1 medium zucchini

12 green beans

2 medium carrots, peeled

6 tablespoons extra-virgin olive oil

3 tablespoons water

$^1/_2$ gallon **Chicken Stock (page 204)** or
   good-quality canned chicken broth

6 ripe tomatoes, peeled and seeded
   (page 217)

30 fresh basil leaves, washed and
   dried

4 medium garlic cloves, peeled

Salt

$^1/_2$ teaspoon freshly ground black
   pepper

1. Cut the leeks, potato, onion, celery, zucchini, green beans, and carrots into ¼-inch dice.

2. In a 6-quart stockpot, combine 3 tablespoons of the olive oil with the water. Add the vegetables and sauté over medium-low heat until all the water evaporates. Do not let the vegetables brown.

3. Add the Chicken Stock and bring to a boil. Cook, uncovered, at a gentle boil for 30 minutes.

4. Meanwhile, in a food processor fitted with the metal blade, put the tomatoes, basil, garlic, and remaining 3 tablespoons olive oil. Pulse until pureed.

5. Stir the puree into the cooked soup. Do not let the soup return to a boil. Season to taste with salt and pepper. Serve the soup hot or cold from a tureen at the dining table or in individual bowls.

Chicken Pot Pie Soup

SERVES 6 TO 8

*T*he flavors of a classic chicken pot pie have been translated into this creamy, chunky soup, in which light-as-air dumplings take the place of a crust. The result is robust enough to become a meal in itself.

2 tablespoons extra-virgin olive oil

2 leeks, trimmed, thoroughly washed, and chopped

1 large onion, peeled and chopped

2 celery stalks, diced

1 large garlic clove, peeled and minced

1/3 cup all-purpose flour

8 cups Chicken Stock (page 204) or good-quality canned chicken broth

2 medium carrots, peeled and cut into 1/2-inch dice

1 pound small white button mushrooms, quartered

1 bag frozen pearl onions, 10 ounces

2 large whole boneless, skinless chicken breasts, trimmed and cut crosswise into thin strips

1 to 2 teaspoons salt

1/2 teaspoon dried tarragon

1/2 teaspoon ground white pepper

1 cup water

1 cup heavy cream

DUMPLINGS

3/4 cup all-purpose flour

3/4 teaspoon baking powder

1/2 teaspoon salt

Pinch of freshly ground black pepper

2 tablespoons unsalted butter, chilled

1 large egg

3 tablespoons milk

1 tablespoon finely chopped fresh parsley, plus more for garnish

1. In a soup pot, heat the oil over medium heat. Add the leeks, onion, celery, and garlic. Sauté, stirring occasionally, until the vegetables are almost tender, about 7 minutes. Sprinkle in the flour and, stirring constantly, cook for about 2 minutes, taking care not to let the flour brown.

2. Remove the pot from the heat and gradually stir in 6 cups of the Chicken Stock. Add the carrots, mushrooms, pearl onions, chicken, salt, tarragon, and white pepper. Return the pan to medium-high heat and bring to a boil, stirring occasionally and skimming off any foam that rises to the surface. Reduce the heat to very low, cover, and simmer for about 30 minutes or until the vegetables and chicken are tender. Meanwhile, in a separate large, shallow pan over medium-high heat, bring the remaining 2 cups of chicken broth and the 1 cup water to a boil.

3. To make the dumplings: In a medium mixing bowl, combine the flour, baking powder, salt, and pepper. With a pastry blender or fork, cut the butter into the flour mixture until it resembles coarse meal. In a measuring cup or small bowl, beat together the egg, milk, and parsley; stir this into the flour mixture until a dough forms.

4. Using a greased teaspoon, gently place rounded teaspoons of dough into the shallow pan of simmering broth. Cook until the dumplings are well risen and cooked through, about 7 minutes. Remove the pan from the heat and set them aside, still floating in the broth, to keep warm and moist until ready to serve.

5. Just before serving, stir the heavy cream into the chicken soup mixture and, if necessary, adjust the thickness of the soup to your liking by stirring in some of the cooking liquid from the dumplings. Adjust the seasonings to taste if necessary. With a slotted spoon, transfer the cooked dumplings to the soup and, over medium heat, return the soup almost to boiling. Serve immediately.

6. To serve the soup, carefully ladle it into warmed soup bowls. Arrange several dumplings on top of each serving. Garnish generously with chopped fresh parsley.

Tortilla Soup

SERVES 6 TO 8

I fell in love with this soup, a Southwestern and Mexican favorite, many years ago on a visit to Texas. Though the flavors are full and robust, its slowly simmered tomato broth base keeps it light and delicate. It has become a popular menu item in all of my **Wolfgang Puck Cafes** and **Wolfgang Puck Expresses. Cook the chicken breast, seasoned to your taste with salt and pepper, using whatever method you like; you can even poach it first in the Chicken Stock or broth, or use an equivalent amount of leftover roast chicken. To prepare ahead, make it earlier in the day through the point at which it is pureed; crisp the tortilla strip garnish as well. The chicken should be sliced and the avocado diced just before you add them to the soup. If you like, you could also garnish the soup with small dollops of Jalapeno Cream (page 32).**

2 ears fresh corn, shucked

4 or 5 large garlic cloves, peeled

1 small onion, peeled, trimmed, and
  quartered

1 small jalapeño chili, stemmed and
  seeded

2 tablespoons corn oil

2 corn tortillas, cut into 1-inch
  squares

2 large ripe tomatoes, peeled and
  seeded (page 217) and coarsely
  chopped

2 tablespoons tomato paste

2 teaspoons ground cumin

8 cups Chicken Stock (page 204) or
  good-quality canned chicken
  broth, heated

Kosher salt

Freshly ground black pepper

GARNISH

2 corn tortillas

1 ripe avocado

1 large whole chicken breast, cooked,
  boned, and skinned

1/2 cup shredded Cheddar cheese

1/4 cup chopped fresh cilantro leaves

1. Using a large, sharp knife, carefully cut the kernels off the corncobs. Set the kernels aside and reserve the cobs.

2. Put the corn kernels, garlic, onion, and jalapeño in a food processor fitted with the metal blade. Pulse the machine until the mixture is coarsely chopped. Set aside.

3. To make the soup: In a large soup pot, heat the oil over low heat. Add the squares of tortilla and cook until they are slightly darkened in color and a little crisp, 2 to 3 minutes. Stir in the chopped corn mixture and sauté just until the vegetables are coated with the oil, about 1 minute. Do not let them brown.

4. Add the tomatoes, tomato paste, and cumin and continue to cook, stirring occasionally, until the mixture is very aromatic, about 10 minutes. Meanwhile, in a separate saucepan, heat the stock or broth. Slowly pour the stock into the vegetable mixture, add the corncobs, and simmer over low heat until the soup is reduced by one third, 15 to 20 minutes.

5. Remove and discard the corncobs. In a blender or food processor, puree the soup in batches until smooth, taking care to avoid splattering. At this point, if you'd like a finer consistency, you can pass the soup through a fine strainer. Return the soup to a clean pot and season to taste with salt and pepper.

6. To prepare the garnish: Preheat the oven to 350°F. Cut the tortillas into thin strips and arrange on a small baking sheet. Bake until the strips are crisp, 10 to 15 minutes. Peel and dice the avocado. Cut the chicken crosswise into thin strips.

7. To serve, add the chicken and avocado to the soup and rewarm over low heat. Ladle the soup into 6 to 8 warmed soup bowls and garnish with the baked tortilla strips, Cheddar cheese, and chopped cilantro. Serve immediately.

Corn Chowder with Littleneck Clams and Jalapeño Cream

SERVES 6 TO 8

•• *Y*ou need farm-fresh corn, preferably no more than a few hours out of the field, and fresh clams in the shell to give this autumn soup its unforgettably sweet, delicate flavor. Simmering the corn cobs in the broth for 30 minutes adds extra flavor.

CORN CHOWDER

3 cups Chicken Stock (page 204) or
   good-quality canned chicken broth

1 cup dry white wine

1 garlic clove, peeled

2 sprigs of fresh thyme

2 pounds (about 4 dozen) littleneck
   clams in the shell, scrubbed clean

4 tablespoons (1/2 stick) unsalted
   butter

1 medium onion, peeled and diced

1 leek, white part only, thoroughly
   washed and diced

1 large carrot, peeled and diced

1 stalk celery, diced

8 ears fresh corn, shucked, kernels
   removed (reserve cobs)

1 1/2 cups heavy cream

Salt

Freshly ground white pepper

Juice of 1/2 small lemon

JALAPEÑO CREAM

1/2 cup heavy cream, whipped

1/4 cup sour cream

1 jalapeño chili, stemmed, cored,
   seeded, and minced

Salt

Freshly ground white pepper

1. To prepare the chowder: In a large soup pot, combine the Chicken Stock, white wine, garlic, and thyme. Bring to a boil over medium-high heat. Add the clams and bring the liquid back to a boil; reduce the heat to a bare simmer, cover the pot, and steam the clams until they have just opened, 3 to 4 minutes.

2. Line a strainer with a double thickness of cheesecloth and place it over a large mixing bowl. Pour the contents of the pot into the strainer. Discard any unopened clams. When the opened clams are cool enough to handle, remove the clams from their shells; discard the shells and set the clam meat aside in a separate bowl.

3. In a 3-quart saucepan over medium heat, melt the butter. Sauté the onion, leek, carrot, and celery until the vegetables are tender but still slightly crisp, about 10 minutes. Pour in the clam liquid and bring to a boil. Add the corncobs and the corn kernels, reserving 1 cup of kernels for a garnish. Simmer for 30 minutes.

4. Remove the cobs and strain the soup into a clean saucepan. Transfer the strained vegetables to a blender or food processor, pour in the cream, and process until coarsely pureed. Stir the puree back into the soup and season lightly to taste with salt and pepper. Bring the soup to a boil, add the reserved clams, and simmer for 1 minute. Season to taste with salt, pepper, and lemon juice. Remove from the heat and keep warm.

5. Meanwhile, prepare the Jalapeño Cream: In a small bowl, combine all the ingredients, seasoning to taste with salt and pepper.

6. Ladle the soup into heated bowls, making sure to distribute the clams evenly. Spoon a little of the Jalapeño Cream into the center of each bowl. Garnish each serving with some of the reserved corn kernels and serve immediately, passing the remaining Jalapeño Cream for each person to add more to taste.

Classic French Onion Soup

■ ■ *Did* you know that Les Halles, Paris's historic and now departed public market, was famed for the onion soup sold in the modest cafés that surrounded it? Not only did the humble soup made from simple ingredients fortify the weary market porters, but it also was a renowned hangover cure for bons vivants after a night on the town. Adding a splash of port makes the slowly simmered soup taste extra-rich, and most of the alcohol in the fortified wine evaporates during simmering. Serve this soup with more French bread, so guests can sop up every last drop.

3 tablespoons safflower oil or olive oil	Salt
4 medium onions, peeled and thinly sliced	Freshly ground black pepper
1/2 cup port	12 slices French bread, about 1/4 inch thick
8 cups Chicken Stock (page 204) or good-quality canned chicken broth	2 cups shredded Swiss cheese
Bouquet garni, made with 1 sprig thyme, 1 bay leaf, 1 celery stalk (page 223)	

1. In a large soup pot over medium-high heat, heat the oil. Add the onions and sauté, stirring frequently and taking care that the onions do not scorch, until golden brown, about 20 minutes.

2. Add the port to the pan and deglaze, stirring and scraping with a wooden spoon to dissolve the pan deposits. Stir in the stock, add the bouquet garni, and season to taste with

salt and pepper. When the liquid reaches a boil, reduce the heat and simmer for about 40 minutes.

3. Meanwhile, arrange the bread slices on a baking sheet and put them in an oven set to 200°F. When the bread slices are dry and crusty, place 1 slice in each of 6 deep ovenproof soup bowls. Set the other slices aside and place the bowls on the baking sheet. Preheat the broiler.

4. Ladle the soup over the bread in each bowl. Top each bowl with 1 more slice of bread and sprinkle with ⅓ cup of the cheese. Place the baking sheet with the bowls under the broiler and broil until the cheese is melted and bubbly, 2 to 3 minutes.

SALADS

Goat Cheese Salad with Arugula and Radicchio

Greek Shrimp Salad

Chinois Chicken Salad

Chino Chopped-Vegetable Salad

Insalata Pantesca

Spago Cucumber Salad

All-American Potato Salad

Goat Cheese Salad with Arugula and Radicchio

*A*ll three of the featured ingredients in this simply made salad arrived on the California cooking scene around the same time in the early 1980s. They work wonderfully together. The tangy richness and smoothness of the goat cheese perfectly balance with the crispness and slightly bitter tastes of the two salad leaves. From among the various types of goat cheese sold in markets today (see photo, opposite) look for a log-shaped, fresh, creamy goat cheese, which will taste fairly mild, and allow about an hour to marinate it. And pick smaller, younger arugula and radicchio leaves; they develop harsher flavors as they mature.

MUSTARD VINAIGRETTE

1 tablespoon Dijon mustard

1 tablespoon finely chopped fresh
    tarragon

1 tablespoon sherry wine vinegar or
    red wine vinegar

Salt

Freshly ground white pepper

1 cup almond oil or extra-virgin olive
    oil (or a mixture of both)

SALAD

4 ounces fresh, creamy log-shaped
    goat cheese, cut into 4 equal slices

1 garlic clove, peeled and crushed

1 1/2 teaspoons fresh thyme leaves

Freshly ground black pepper

1/4 cup extra-virgin olive oil

2 small heads radicchio

2 bunches of arugula

1. To prepare the vinaigrette: In a small bowl, stir together the mustard, tarragon, and vinegar. Stir in salt and pepper to taste. Whisking continually, slowly pour in the oil. Taste and adjust the seasonings, even adding a little more mustard or vinegar if you like. Cover and set aside.

2. In a bowl, put the cheese, garlic clove, and 1 teaspoon of the thyme leaves. Add some black pepper to taste. Pour the olive oil over the cheese, cover, and leave to marinate at room temperature for up to 1 hour.

3. Before serving, separate the radicchio and arugula leaves, rinse them well with cold water, and dry them thoroughly in a salad spinner or with paper towels. Put the leaves in a salad bowl and toss them with enough of the vinaigrette to coat them lightly. Divide the greens among 4 large salad plates.

4. Heat a nonstick sauté pan until very hot and add 2 tablespoons of the olive oil in which the goat cheese has marinated. Reduce the heat to medium, add the cheese slices, and sauté them for 30 seconds per side, turning with a spatula. Transfer a slice of warm cheese to the center of each salad, garnish the cheese with the remaining thyme leaves and a little more of the vinaigrette if you like, and serve immediately.

Greek Shrimp Salad

*A*dding quickly poached shrimp tossed with their own yogurt-and-lemon dressing transforms this from an ordinary **Greek** salad into an extraordinary one that features the best of the Mediterranean, both land and sea. **Add some love and it's even better!**

16 large shrimp, peeled and deveined
(page 233), cut in half horizontally

SHRIMP DRESSING

1/2 cup plain yogurt

2 tablespoons fresh lemon juice

2 tablespoons peeled, seeded, and
finely diced cucumber

1 tablespoon minced red onion

1 tablespoon minced fresh dill leaves

1 teaspoon minced garlic

Pinch of cayenne pepper

Kosher salt

Freshly ground black pepper

SALAD

1 romaine heart, torn into bite-size
pieces

4 cups mixed baby lettuces, washed
and dried

1/2 cup each red and yellow bell
peppers, cored, seeded, trimmed,
and cut into 1-inch dice

1/2 cup Caramelized Onions (page 160)

1/2 cup Kalamata olives, pitted
(page 231)

1 small cucumber, peeled, seeded,
quartered, and cut into 1/2-inch
slices

1 cup halved yellow pear and Sweet
100 cherry tomatoes

1/2 cup freshly grated Parmesan
cheese

1 cup crumbled feta cheese

1 cup Greek Salad Dressing (page 228)

Kosher salt

Freshly ground black pepper

1/4 cup pine nuts, toasted (page 221)

Sprigs of fresh dill

1. First, prepare the shrimp: Bring a small saucepan of lightly salted water to a boil. Reduce the heat to a simmer, add the shrimp, and cook them just until they turn pink and opaque, 1 to 2 minutes. Drain well, transfer to a bowl, cover, and refrigerate.

2. To make the dressing: In a medium bowl, whisk together the yogurt, lemon juice, cucum-

ber, red onion, dill, and garlic until well blended. Season with cayenne and salt and pepper to taste. Cover and refrigerate.

3. Just before serving, in a large mixing bowl, combine the romaine, baby lettuces, bell peppers, Caramelized Onions, olives, cucumber, tomatoes, cheeses, and Greek Salad Dressing. Toss until the ingredients are coated well. Season to taste with salt and pepper. Divide the mixture among 4 chilled salad plates, mounding it attractively.

4. With a whisk, briefly restir the Shrimp Dressing until smooth. Add the shrimp to the dressing and toss to coat them well. Arrange 8 shrimp halves around each salad mound. Top with pine nuts and garnish with dill sprigs.

Chinois Chicken Salad

*S*ince we first opened **Chinois** in Santa Monica in 1983, this salad has been one of the most popular items on the menu. Guests at all our **Wolfgang Puck Cafes** and **Wolfgang Puck Expresses** love it, too. The combination of roast chicken, crisp vegetables, and a rich, spicy, tangy vinaigrette is a perfect example of the California-Asian fusion cooking for which **Chinois** is famous. To streamline preparation, you can roast the chicken a day ahead and keep it refrigerated, either whole or shredded, until you put the salad together.

CHINESE MUSTARD VINAIGRETTE

2 teaspoons dry Chinese or English
   (Colman's) mustard

1/4 cup rice wine vinegar

1 teaspoon soy sauce

2 tablespoons light sesame oil

Salt

Freshly ground black pepper

2 to 3 tablespoons peanut oil

CHICKEN SALAD

1 whole chicken, 3 pounds, cavity
   filled with finely diced celery,
   carrot, onion, garlic, bay leaf,
   thyme, salt, and pepper

4 tablespoons (1/2 stick) unsalted
   butter, melted

2 small heads or 1 medium head napa
   cabbage

1 cup 1/4-inch julienne romaine lettuce

10 snow peas, cut into 1/4-inch
   julienne strips

1 tablespoon black sesame seeds or
   toasted (page 222) white sesame
   seeds

1. To prepare the vinaigrette: Put all the vinaigrette ingredients, except the peanut oil, in a blender or food processor and blend until smooth. With the machine running, slowly pour in the peanut oil. Taste the dressing and adjust the seasonings to taste.

2. Preheat the oven to 425°F.

3. Put the chicken on a rack in a roasting pan and coat it with some of the butter. Roast until done, about 1½ hours, basting every 15 or 20 minutes with the butter and pan drippings.

To test for doneness, pierce the thickest part of the thigh with a sharp knife tip or skewer: the juices should run clear. Remove from the oven and let the chicken rest.

4. Select 4 to 8 nice-looking leaves from the napa cabbage and reserve them. Slice the remaining cabbage crosswise into ¼-inch julienne strips.

5. Shred the meat from the breasts and thighs of the chicken. (Use the remaining meat and the carcass to make Chicken Stock, page 204.)

6. In a mixing bowl, combine the chicken, shredded cabbage, romaine, and snow peas. Toss with enough of the vinaigrette to coat the ingredients well.

7. Arrange the reserved napa cabbage leaves around the edge of a large serving plate or platter and mound the salad in the center. Sprinkle with the sesame seeds. Alternatively, mound the salad atop the whole reserved leaves on individual serving plates.

Chino Chopped-Vegetable Salad

*W*hat tastes better and lighter on a hot summer day than a fresh vegetable salad? **No one I know grows better vegetables than the Chino family on their organic farm in Rancho Santa Fe north of San Diego. If you live in Southern California, their wonderful place is worth a special visit. Or go to your own local farm stand or farmers' market to buy the absolutely freshest ingredients to make this recipe. Be creative, too, adding or substituting other fresh vegetables, such as baby peas, diced snow peas, or diced summer squash.**

DIJON MUSTARD VINAIGRETTE

1 tablespoon Dijon mustard

3 tablespoons sherry wine vinegar

1/2 cup extra-virgin olive oil

1/2 cup almond or safflower oil

Salt

Freshly ground white pepper

SALAD

1 tablespoon extra-virgin olive oil

1/2 cup diced fresh artichoke hearts
   (page 232)

Salt

Freshly ground white pepper

1/2 cup diced carrots

1/2 cup diced green beans

1/2 cup diced red onion

1/2 cup diced radicchio

1/2 cup fresh corn kernels

1/2 cup diced celery

1 small vine-ripened tomato

1 small ripe Hass-style avocado

4 teaspoons grated Parmesan cheese

1 cup mixed greens of your choice
   (curly endive, chicory, baby
   lettuce), cut or torn into bite-size
   pieces

1. To prepare the vinaigrette: In a small bowl, combine the mustard and vinegar. Whisking continuously, slowly pour in the oils. Season to taste with salt and pepper and set aside.

2. To prepare the salad: In a small skillet, heat the olive oil. Season the diced artichokes lightly with salt and pepper and sauté until al dente, tender but still firm, about 3 minutes. Transfer to a large bowl and let cool.

3. Bring a large pot of salted water to a boil. To blanch the carrots and green beans, put them in a wire sieve, set the sieve inside the pot of boiling water, and cook until the vegetables

are al dente, tender but still firm, 2 to 3 minutes. Plunge the sieve of vegetables into a bowl of cold water to stop the cooking process. Drain the vegetables, let them cool, and add them to the artichokes. Add the onion, radicchio, corn, and celery.

4. When ready to serve, peel, seed, and dice the tomato (page 217) and pit, peel, and dice the avocado (page 232), adding them both to the other vegetables. Briefly whisk the dressing again. Reserving a few tablespoons of the vinaigrette, add the rest to the vegetables and toss to coat them well. Sprinkle on the grated Parmesan and toss again. Adjust the seasonings to taste.

5. Toss the greens with the reserved dressing and season with salt and pepper to taste. Divide the salad greens among 4 salad plates. Mound the chopped salad on top and serve immediately.

Insalata Pantesca

SERVES 4 TO 6

A perfect accompaniment to seafood, poultry, or meat grilled with olive oil and fresh herbs, this rustic tomato salad is inspired by the world-famous caper berries of Pantelleria, an Italian island in the Mediterranean just fifty miles off the coast of Tunisia. You can make it with regular sun-ripened tomatoes if that's all you have available. But using three or more different colors of heirloom tomatoes from the farmers' market will result in a salad that is not only more beautiful but even more delicious. The caper berries used to garnish the salad are the pickled immature fruit of the same Mediterranean flowering shrub whose buds become capers.

1/2 pound fingerling potatoes

2 small red onions, peeled and thinly sliced

8 medium red heirloom tomatoes, cored and cut into 1-inch cubes

4 medium green heirloom tomatoes, cored and cut into 1-inch cubes

4 medium yellow heirloom tomatoes, cored and cut into 2-inch cubes

1/2 cup green olives (preferably Picholine), pitted (page 231)

2 tablespoons capers, drained

2 tablespoons Champagne vinegar

1/2 teaspoon salt

1 teaspoon freshly ground black pepper

2 tablespoons minced fresh oregano leaves

1/2 cup extra-virgin olive oil

Lemon juice, to taste

1 cup caper berries, for garnish

1. Put the potatoes in a large pot of salted water. Bring to a boil over high heat and continue boiling until the potatoes are tender, about 15 minutes. Drain the potatoes and leave them to cool to room temperature. Peel and cut each potato into 4 to 6 pieces and put them in a medium bowl. Add the red onions, tomatoes, olives, and capers.

2. In another bowl, combine the vinegar, salt, pepper, and oregano. Whisking continuously, slowly pour in the olive oil. Pour this dressing over the potato-tomato mixture. Adjust the seasonings to taste with lemon juice.

3. Mound the salad on individual serving plates and garnish with caper berries.

46 ▪ LIVE, LOVE, EAT!

Spago Cucumber Salad

*I*nspired by the traditional Japanese cucumber salad known as *sunomono,* this crisp, cool side dish goes well with shrimp or other seafood, as well as chicken. Long, slender Japanese cucumbers do not need to be seeded, so you can slice them just as they are. English cucumbers can be substituted, but you'll need to halve them lengthwise and scoop out the seeds with your finger or a teaspoon (as shown below) before slicing them into thin half-moons.

2 cups thinly sliced Japanese
   cucumbers

1 teaspoon salt

1/4 cup rice wine vinegar

1 tablespoon sugar

1 tablespoon soy sauce

1 teaspoon sesame oil

2 teaspoons sesame seeds

1. In a large bowl, thoroughly toss together the cucumbers and salt. Add the rice wine vinegar, sugar, soy sauce, and sesame oil and mix well. Sprinkle with sesame seeds and toss again.

2. Cover the salad and set it aside at room temperature or in the refrigerator to marinate for about 20 minutes. Taste and adjust the seasonings before serving. Divide among 4 chilled plates, mounding the cucumber salad.

All-American Potato Salad

I may be Austrian by birth and by accent, but I'm an American citizen. And as an American, I know this to be a definitive version of the kind of summertime potato salad you'll want to serve at a **Fourth of July** or **Labor Day** cookout. You can either leave the skins on for a little more texture and color or remove them if you prefer a neater look. Remember not to let this mayonnaise-based salad stay out too long in the hot sun!

2 pounds Yukon gold potatoes or other waxy boiling potatoes

3 hard-boiled eggs, finely chopped

1/2 cup mayonnaise, plus more to taste

1/2 medium yellow onion, finely diced

2 stalks celery, finely diced

Kosher salt

Freshly ground black pepper

Sugar, to taste

1. Put the potatoes in a large pot of salted water. Bring them to a boil over high heat and continue boiling until the potatoes are tender when pierced with a sharp knife, about 20 minutes. Drain the potatoes and leave them to cool to room temperature. If you prefer, peel them.

2. Cut each potato into 1-inch chunks and put them in a mixing bowl. Add the eggs, mayonnaise, onion, and celery. With a large spoon or rubber spatula, fold the ingredients together until well mixed, taking care not to break up the potato chunks, and adding more mayonnaise if you would like a creamier salad. Season to taste with salt, pepper, and a little sugar.

PIZZA AND PASTA

Spicy Chicken Pizza

Pizza with Smoked Salmon and Caviar

Four Seasons Pizza

Calzone with Artichoke Hearts and Porcini Mushrooms

Fettuccine Wolf-fredo with Grilled Chicken

Pasta Puttanesca

My Favorite Tomato Sauce

Angel Hair with Tomato Sauce

Hearty Beef Bolognese

Classic Beef Lasagne

My Special Spaghetti and Meatballs

Bucatini with Mussels, Clams, and Oven-Dried Tomatoes

Pumpkin Ravioli

White Corn Agnolotti

Wild Mushroom Risotto

Spicy Chicken Pizza

*I*f you live in **Southern California** as I do, it's impossible not to be influenced by **Mexican** and **Southwestern** cooking. Those cuisines inspired the topping for one of the most popular menu items at my **Wolfgang Puck Cafes** and **Expresses**. The combination of marinated chicken, chilies, tomatoes, and roasted vegetables makes a wonderful, hearty pizza that's equally perfect for a family meal or for a special dinner party.

MARINATED CHICKEN

About 1¼ pounds skinned and boned
    uncooked chicken, cut into bite-
    size cubes (4 cups)

½ cup plus 1 tablespoon extra-virgin
    olive oil

3½ tablespoons fresh lime juice

2 large jalapeño chilies, stemmed,
    seeded, and minced

1 garlic clove, peeled and minced

1 tablespoon chopped fresh cilantro
    leaves

Kosher salt

TOPPINGS

3 tablespoons extra-virgin olive oil

1 slender Asian eggplant, cut into
    ½-inch cubes

Salt

Freshly ground black pepper

1 small red or yellow bell pepper,
    stemmed, seeded, and thinly sliced

2 cups shredded mozzarella cheese
    (about 8 ounces)

2 cups shredded Fontina cheese
    (about 8 ounces)

6 Roma tomatoes (about 1 pound),
    cored and trimmed, thinly sliced

Caramelized Onions (page 160)

Pizza Dough (page 211)

1. To marinate the chicken: Arrange the cubed chicken in a shallow medium bowl and toss with the marinade ingredients, using ½ cup of the olive oil. Season lightly with salt, cover with plastic wrap, and marinate for about 1 hour, refrigerated.

2. In a skillet or sauté pan large enough to hold the chicken in one layer, heat the remaining 1 tablespoon of oil. Remove the chicken from the marinade with a slotted spoon. Add the chicken to the skillet and sauté it just until browned on all sides. Do not overcook. Remove from the skillet with a slotted spoon and set aside.

3. To prepare the toppings: Heat 2 tablespoons of the olive oil in a medium skillet over medium-high heat. Add the eggplant cubes and sauté until al dente, 3 to 4 minutes. Season lightly with salt and pepper, drain, and set aside. In the same skillet, heat the remaining 1 tablespoon of oil. Add the bell pepper and sauté until al dente, about 3 minutes. Season lightly with salt and pepper and set aside. Assemble all the remaining topping ingredients near your work surface.

4. Place a pizza stone on the middle rack of the oven and preheat the oven to 500°F. Lightly flour the work surface and stretch or roll out the dough to make two 10-inch or four 8-inch rounds, with the rim a little thicker than the inner circle. Transfer the pizza dough one at a time to a pizza paddle or rimless cookie sheet and top it.

5. To top the pizza, sprinkle on one half or one fourth of the mozzarella and Fontina. Arrange tomato slices, eggplant, peppers, Caramelized Onions, and cooked chicken on top. Slide the pizza onto the baking stone. Repeat with the remaining pizzas and toppings, baking in batches if necessary. Bake each pizza until its rim is nicely browned and the cheese is bubbly, 10 to 12 minutes.

6. Transfer the pizza to a firm surface and cut into slices with a pizza cutter or a very sharp knife. Serve immediately.

Pizza with Smoked Salmon and Caviar

*W*hen I opened the original Spago in 1982, this quickly became its signature pizza. Because of the toppings' similarity to popular bagel companions, I soon nicknamed it the "Jewish pizza"! At the new Spago Beverly Hills, it's not listed on the menu, but all the regulars know they can get one any time they want. And it's now a regular menu item in all my **Wolfgang Puck Cafes**. In the evening, a glass of champagne makes a perfect partner for the pizza; if you serve it for brunch, feel free to substitute mimosas or a good cup of coffee. If you feel decadent, you can top the pizza with sevruga, beluga, or osetra caviar; less expensive salmon roe or just a scattering of chopped fresh chives are also elegant. To make the pizza ahead, bake it for just 5 minutes in step 2 below; then, just before serving, complete the baking and top the pizza.

6 ounces **Pizza Dough** (page 211)

1 tablespoon **Chili and Garlic Oil** (page 225)

1/4 cup thinly sliced red onion

2 tablespoons **Dill Cream** (page 226)

2 1/2 ounces thinly sliced smoked salmon

1 teaspoon chopped fresh chives

1 tablespoon sevruga caviar, optional

1. Place a pizza stone on the middle rack of the oven and preheat the oven to 500°F.

2. On a lightly floured surface, stretch or roll out the dough into an 8-inch circle, with the outer edge a little thicker than the inner circle. Brush the dough with the oil and arrange the onion over the pizza. Slide a pizza paddle or rimless baking sheet under the pizza and then slide the pizza onto the pizza stone. Bake until the crust is golden brown, 6 to 8 minutes.

3. With the pizza paddle or a large spatula, carefully remove the pizza from the oven and set it on a cutting board. Use a knife, an icing spatula, or the back of a spoon to spread the Dill Cream over the inner circle. Arrange the slices of salmon so that they cover the entire pizza, slightly overlapping the raised rim. Sprinkle the chopped chives over the salmon. Using a pizza cutter or a large sharp knife, cut the pizza into 4 or 6 slices. If you like, spoon a little caviar in the center of each slice. Serve immediately.

Four Seasons Pizza

*I*talians call this style of pizza "Four Seasons" because its surface is divided by strips of dough into four distinct sections, each one featuring an ingredient that represents a different time of year. My version features fresh tomatoes for summer, prosciutto for fall, clams for winter, and little button mushrooms for springtime. Have fun coming up with your own favorite combinations. They don't even all have to come from different seasons! You can prepare the toppings and refrigerate them several hours ahead, so they're ready for final assembly and baking.

1/2 pound Manila or littleneck clams

1 cup dry white wine

1 shallot, finely chopped

2 cups shredded mozzarella cheese
   (about 8 ounces)

2 cups shredded Fontina cheese
   (about 8 ounces)

3 tablespoons extra-virgin olive oil

6 ounces button mushrooms, sliced

Salt

Freshly ground black pepper

1 tomato

8 thin slices prosciutto

Pizza Dough (page 211)

1 1/2 cups My Favorite Tomato Sauce
   (page 63)

2 tablespoons shredded fresh basil
   leaves

1 tablespoon grated Parmesan
   cheese

1. Scrub the clams thoroughly clean under cold running water. In a medium saucepan, bring the wine and shallot to a boil over medium-high heat. Add the clams and cook, covered, until they open, 3 to 4 minutes. Discard any unopened clams. When the clams are cool enough to handle, shell them and set aside.

2. Place a pizza stone on the middle rack of the oven and preheat the oven to 500°F.

3. Prepare the remaining toppings. In a bowl, toss together the mozzarella and Fontina. In a small sauté pan over high heat, heat the olive oil and sauté the mushrooms until golden, about 5 minutes. Season with salt and pepper and transfer to a plate to cool. Cut the tomato into at least 6 thin slices. Cut the prosciutto into thin julienne strips.

4. To assemble the pizzas: Divide the dough into 4 equal balls. On a lightly floured work surface, stretch or roll out a ball of dough into a 10- to 12-inch circle, with the outer edge a

little thicker than the inner circle. Repeat with 2 additional balls. Divide the last dough ball into 6 pieces, and roll each piece into an even 10-inch-long strip. Spread the tomato sauce evenly within the rim of each pizza dough. Scatter the cheeses evenly on top. Carefully place 2 strips of dough over each pizza to divide it into 4 equal quarters, pinching the end of each strip to the rim to seal it. Garnish each of the 4 quarters of each pizza with a different topping: one with tomato slices, one with clams, one with sautéed mushrooms, and one with prosciutto.

5. Slide a pizza paddle or a rimless baking sheet under a pizza and then slide the pizza onto the pizza stone. Repeat with the remaining pizzas as space allows, baking the pizzas in batches if necessary. Bake each pizza until its crust is golden brown, 6 to 7 minutes. Remove the pizza from the oven and transfer it to a serving plate. Sprinkle basil over the tomato section and grated Parmesan over the mushrooms. Serve immediately.

Calzone with Artichoke Hearts and Porcini Mushrooms

MAKES 4 CALZONES

*T*he Italian word *calzone* translates as pantaloons, the kind of long, baggy underwear you might find in antique fashion illustrations. Squint your eyes a little, and stretch your imagination, and you just might see how one of these filled pizza turnovers looks like one leg of a pair of pantaloons. The shape calls for a robust, generous filling like this mixture of firm, flavorful vegetables. If you can't find wonderfully meaty fresh porcini mushrooms, substitute another flavorful type, such as fresh cremini or shiitake, or just regular button mushrooms. Add meat if you wish, such as strips of ham or prosciutto, pieces of sautéed bacon or Italian pancetta, or chunks or slices of cooked or cured sausage.

Pizza Dough (page 211)

2 tablespoons extra-virgin olive oil

2 large artichoke hearts (page 232), very thinly sliced

$1^1/_2$ cups fresh porcini mushrooms, sliced if large

Salt

Freshly ground pepper

2 tablespoons Chili and Garlic Oil (page 225)

2 cups shredded mozzarella cheese

1 cup shredded Fontina cheese

2 tablespoons chopped Double-Blanched Garlic (page 220)

1 tablepoon chopped fresh thyme, plus 4 sprigs for garnish

2 tablespoons unsalted butter, melted

2 tablespoons freshly grated Parmesan cheese

1. Place a pizza stone on the middle rack of the oven and preheat the oven to 500°F. Divide the pizza dough into 4 equal pieces.

2. Place a large sauté pan over high heat. Add the olive oil and, when it is hot, add the artichoke hearts and mushrooms and sauté them until they are tender and just beginning to color, 5 to 7 minutes. Season to taste with salt and pepper. Pour off any excess oil, transfer the vegetables to a bowl, and let them cool.

3. On a lightly floured work surface, stretch or roll out each dough ball into a 9-inch circle.

Brush to within 1 inch of the edge with Chili and Garlic Oil. On half of the dough's surface, still leaving a 1-inch border, spread one fourth of both the mozzarella and Fontina. Top with one fourth each of the artichoke-mushroom mixture, the garlic, and the chopped thyme. Assemble the remaining calzones in the same way.

4. Moisten the edges of the 4 dough circles with water. Loosely fold the untopped half of the dough, trapping as much air inside as possible, over the filling and firmly press the edges together to seal. With the tines of a table fork, press down all along the sealed edges to crimp them.

5. One at a time, slide a floured pizza paddle or rimless baking sheet under a calzone and transfer it to the heated pizza stone in the oven. Repeat and, if necessary, do the calzones in batches. Bake until the calzones are puffed and golden brown, about 12 minutes. Slide the paddle or baking sheet under the calzones and remove them from the oven onto heated serving plates. Brush with melted butter, sprinkle with Parmesan, and garnish with thyme sprigs before serving immediately.

Fettuccine Wolf-fredo with Grilled Chicken

I've always loved the pasta dish known as fettuccine Alfredo, invented at a restaurant of the same name in the heart of Rome. Of course, I couldn't resist tinkering with the classic formula for its creamy Parmesan sauce. I added lots of shallots, garlic, thyme, the Italian bacon known as pancetta, and a hint of fiery crushed red pepper. Soon, the chefs in my **Wolfgang Puck Cafes**, where this has become hugely popular, were joking that the sauce ought to be renamed Wolf-fredo. So we did. Feel free to play with the recipe yourself! And don't worry that it looks a little long. It's really easy, and you can even make the sauce ahead of time and gently reheat it before serving.

PARMESAN CREAM SAUCE

2 cups dry white wine

1/2 cup chopped shallots

2 teaspoons whole white peppercorns

2 small sprigs of fresh thyme

2 cups **Chicken Stock (page 204)** or
    good-quality canned chicken broth

3 cups heavy cream

1 1/2 cups freshly grated Parmesan
    cheese

1 teaspoon chopped fresh thyme
    leaves

1 teaspoon chopped fresh oregano
    leaves

Salt

Freshly ground white pepper

GRILLED CHICKEN

4 boneless, skinless chicken breast
    halves

Extra-virgin olive oil

Salt

Freshly ground black pepper

PASTA

1 pound fettuccine pasta, fresh
    (page 209) or dried

2 tablespoons extra-virgin olive oil

2 teaspoons minced garlic

1/2 cup diced pancetta

1 teaspoon chopped fresh thyme
leaves

1 teaspoon chopped fresh oregano
leaves

1/2 cup Chicken Stock (page 204) or
good-quality canned chicken broth

2 tablespoons chopped fresh flat-leaf
parsley

1/8 to 1/4 teaspoon crushed red pepper
flakes

Salt

Freshly ground black pepper

Thyme or oregano sprigs for garnish

1. First, make the Parmesan Cream Sauce: In a large saucepan over medium-high heat, combine the white wine, shallots, peppercorns, and thyme. Cook until the wine has evaporated to a few tablespoons, 15 to 20 minutes.

2. Add the Chicken Stock and continue to cook until the liquid reduces by half, about 10 minutes more. Add the cream and cook for several minutes more, until the sauce is slightly thickened. Strain the sauce through a fine-mesh wire sieve into a mixing bowl.

3. Working in batches if necessary, combine the strained sauce with the grated Parmesan, thyme, and oregano, blending until smooth. Strain the sauce once more through the sieve. Season to taste with salt and freshly ground white pepper. Set aside.

4. Preheat the grill or broiler. At the same time, bring a large pot of salted water to a boil.

5. Brush the chicken breasts with olive oil and season with salt and black pepper. Grill or broil them until done, 4 to 5 minutes per side.

6. Meanwhile, cook the fettuccine in the pot of boiling water until al dente, tender but still chewy, following the manufacturer's suggested cooking time. (Fresh pasta will cook in no more than half the time that dried takes.)

7. While the chicken and pasta are cooking, heat the 2 tablespoons of olive oil in a large skillet over medium-high heat. Add the garlic and cook until fragrant, about 1 minute. Add the pancetta and chopped thyme and oregano and sauté about 2 minutes more. Stir in the Chicken Stock and stir and scrape with a wooden spoon to deglaze the pan. Stir in the prepared Parmesan Cream Sauce. Cook only until heated through. Remove 1 cup of the sauce and set aside.

8. When the fettuccine is done, drain it and add it immediately to the sauce in the skillet

along with the chopped parsley and red pepper flakes. Toss thoroughly and adjust the seasoning to taste with salt and pepper, if necessary.

9. Cut each chicken breast crosswise on a slant into slices. Mound the fettuccine on heated plates or in pasta serving bowls. Fan out each sliced chicken breast alongside or on top of the pasta and drizzle it with the reserved sauce. Garnish each plate with a thyme or oregano sprig and serve immediately.

Pasta Puttanesca

I guess this classic sauce's combination of lusty ingredients—garlic, anchovies, red pepper flakes, capers, and olives—inspired Italians to name it for women of ill repute. There's no arguing that people who love pasta puttanesca are absolutely passionate about it. Serve the quickly made sauce with your favorite dried pasta. Spaghetti, linguine, or penne are popular choices.

1/4 cup extra-virgin olive oil	1/4 cup Niçoise olives, pitted
2 tablespoons minced garlic	1 teaspoon minced fresh oregano
6 anchovy fillets, chopped	16 fresh basil leaves, torn into pieces
4 pounds tomatoes, peeled, seeded, and diced (page 217)	2 tablespoons minced fresh parsley leaves
1/2 teaspoon red pepper flakes	Salt
3/4 pound dry pasta	Freshly ground black pepper
2 tablespoons capers, drained	Freshly grated Parmesan cheese

1. Bring a large pot of salted water to a boil.

2. Meanwhile, in a large sauté pan, heat the olive oil over medium heat. Add the garlic and sauté 1 minute. Add the anchovy fillets, about three quarters of the tomatoes, and the red pepper flakes. When the tomatoes begin to release their liquid and boil, reduce the heat to a simmer and cook, stirring occasionally, for 15 minutes.

3. As soon as the salted water is boiling, add the pasta and boil until al dente, tender but still chewy, following the manufacturer's suggested cooking time.

4. As soon as the pasta is done, drain it and add it, still slightly dripping, to the sauté pan, along with the remaining tomatoes and the capers, olives, and oregano. Toss to mix and coat the pasta with the sauce. Remove the pan from the heat, add the basil and parsley, and season to taste with salt and pepper, tossing lightly.

5. Divide the pasta among heated serving plates and serve immediately, passing the Parmesan cheese for guests to add to taste.

My Favorite Tomato Sauce

MAKES ABOUT 5 CUPS, 4 SERVINGS

A classic Italian-style red sauce, this easy recipe is extremely versatile. Use it often for a simple pasta meal, or in place of Hearty Beef Bolognese sauce for lasagne (page 65). Or leave out the butter and try it as a pizza sauce. If you want more texture, simply don't strain the sauce. Substitute canned vegetable broth for the Chicken Stock if you'd like a meat-free version.

1/4 cup extra-virgin olive oil

2 small onions, peeled, trimmed, and minced

6 garlic cloves, minced

2 tablespoons tomato paste

4 pounds Roma tomatoes, peeled, seeded, and diced (page 217)

2 cups Chicken Stock (page 204) or good-quality canned chicken broth, heated

12 to 16 fresh basil leaves, washed and dried

12 tablespoons (1 1/2 sticks) unsalted butter, cut into small pieces

Kosher salt

Freshly ground black pepper

1. In a large saucepan, heat the olive oil over medium-high heat. Add the onion and sauté until soft, about 5 minutes. Add the garlic and cook 1 minute longer. Add the tomato paste and then the tomatoes, cook for 2 to 3 minutes, and then pour in the Chicken Stock. Simmer briskly until the sauce is thick, 20 to 30 minutes. For a finer consistency, pass the sauce through a wire-mesh sieve into a clean saucepan.

2. Stack the basil leaves, roll them up lengthwise, and cut across the roll very thinly to make a chiffonade (page 229). Stir the basil into the sauce. Whisk in the butter piece by piece, then season to taste with salt and pepper. Keep warm.

Angel Hair with Tomato Sauce

*J*ust by adding some extra basil to My Favorite Tomato Sauce, you can turn dried pasta from the supermarket into an authentic-tasting Italian dish. Cooking the pasta briefly in the sauce helps to blend the flavors, a trick Italian home cooks know. The presentation, simply achieved by coiling the pasta strands around a fork, helps to make humble ingredients look like a special occasion.

5 cups My Favorite Tomato Sauce
   (page 63)

1 pound dried angel hair pasta

1/2 cup julienne of fresh basil
   (page 229)

1/2 cup chiffonade of fresh basil
   (page 229)

1. In a large saucepan over medium-high heat, bring My Favorite Tomato Sauce almost to a boil, stirring occasionally. At the same time, bring another large saucepan or pot of salted water to a boil.

2. Add the pasta to the boiling water and cook until al dente, tender but still chewy, following the manufacturer's suggested cooking time.

3. Stir the julienne of fresh basil into the tomato sauce. As soon as the pasta is done, drain it and transfer immediately to the tomato sauce, stirring in the pasta. Cook the sauce and pasta together for 1 minute.

4. Divide the pasta into four equal portions. Using tongs or a carving fork, twirl each portion in the center of each serving bowl into a neatly swirled mound. Spoon the remaining sauce from the pan over the pasta and garnish with the chiffonade of fresh basil.

Hearty Beef Bolognese

MAKES ABOUT 7 CUPS, 4 TO 6 SERVINGS

*S*erve this authentic, slowly simmered meat sauce, a specialty of Bologna, Italy, with spaghetti, linguine, or fettuccine. Or layer it with sheets of pasta or broad lasagne noodles for the classic, hearty layered and baked pasta dish (page 67). The sauce can be made ahead and refrigerated in a covered container for 2 to 3 days or frozen in an airtight container for up to 3 months.

6 tablespoons extra-virgin olive oil

1 pound lean ground beef

1 teaspoon salt

1/4 teaspoon freshly ground black pepper

2 teaspoons minced shallots

1 teaspoon minced garlic

1/2 cup dry red wine

5 pounds Roma tomatoes, cored, peeled, seeded, and chopped (page 217)

2 tablespoons tomato paste

3 tablespoons sugar

1 bouquet garni (page 223), made up of 2 sprigs each rosemary, basil, parsley, 1 sprig oregano, 2 bay leaves, and 1 tablespoon black peppercorns

1 medium onion, peeled and finely diced

1 medium carrot, peeled and finely diced

1 medium celery stalk, trimmed and finely diced

2 cups Chicken Stock (page 204) or good-quality canned chicken broth

1. In a large saucepan over medium-high heat, heat 3 tablespoons of the olive oil. Add the ground beef and sauté until evenly browned, 5 to 7 minutes, breaking up the large chunks of meat with a wooden spoon as they cook. Season with salt and pepper. Add the shallots and garlic and continue sautéing until the shallots are soft, about 3 minutes more.

2. Add the red wine and deglaze, stirring and scraping to dissolve the pan deposits. Continue cooking until almost all liquid has been absorbed or evaporated.

3. Add the chopped tomatoes, tomato paste, sugar, and bouquet garni. Bring the mixture to a boil. Reduce the heat and simmer, covered, for about 45 minutes, stirring frequently.

4. Meanwhile, in a small skillet over medium-high heat, heat the remaining 3 tablespoons

olive oil. Add the onion, carrot, and celery and sauté until the onion is translucent, about 4 minutes.

5. Stir the sautéed vegetables along with the Chicken Stock into the meat sauce. Continue to simmer, stirring occasionally, until the sauce is thickened and rich-tasting, about 30 minutes more. Adjust the seasonings to taste with a little more salt, pepper, or sugar, if necessary.

Classic Beef Lasagne

SERVES 8

*Y*ou can use fresh or dried pasta, cut into the wide ribbons known as lasagne, for this favorite Italian comfort food. They are layered with a rich beef Bolognese sauce and a creamy ricotta filling and topped off with mozzarella cheese to make a robust, heartwarming dish. After baking, remember to allow 10 minutes for the lasagne to rest at room temperature before serving; this step lets the layers settle, so you can cut out the portions much more neatly.

6 cups Hearty Beef Bolognese
(page 65)

2 cups ricotta cheese

3/4 cup freshly grated Parmesan
cheese, plus more for serving

1/2 cup mascarpone cheese

1 large egg, beaten

1 pound dried lasagne noodles or
fresh pasta sheets (page 209)

Extra-virgin olive oil

1 1/2 cups shredded mozzarella cheese

Chopped fresh Italian parsley,
for garnish

Freshly ground black pepper

1. Prepare the Hearty Beef Bolognese and set it aside to cool.

2. In a large bowl, stir together the ricotta cheese, ½ cup of the Parmesan, the mascarpone, and the egg. Cover and refrigerate.

3. Meanwhile, bring a large pot of salted water to a boil. If using dried lasagne noodles, add them to the water and cook until al dente, tender but still chewy, following the manufacturer's suggested cooking time. Drain the noodles and immediately plunge them into a bowl of iced water to stop cooking. Remove the noodles from the water and lay them on a

lightly oiled baking sheet, separating the layers of noodles with lightly oiled plastic wrap. If using fresh pasta sheets, cook only 2 or 3 sheets at a time and follow the same directions for cooling and layering them given above.

4. Preheat the oven to 375°F. With the olive oil, lightly brush a 13 by 9 by 3-inch baking dish. Lay about 3 cooked lasagne noodles lengthwise side by side on the bottom of the dish to cover it. Cover the noodles with a layer of Bolognese sauce, about 2 cups, and top the sauce with another layer of noodles. Cover this layer of pasta with half of the ricotta mixture. Add another layer each of noodles, Bolognese, noodles, and ricotta. Top with a final layer of noodles and Bolognese sauce, and then sprinkle the top with the mozzarella and Parmesan cheeses.

5. Bake the lasagne until it is heated through, browned, and bubbly, about 45 minutes. Remove it from the oven and let it rest at room temperature for 10 minutes before cutting and serving. Generously sprinkle each portion with chopped fresh parsley. Pass more grated Parmesan cheese and a pepper grinder for guests to add to their servings to taste.

My Special Spaghetti and Meatballs

*..W*hat makes this version of the Italian standby so special? You'll find that the meatballs are incredibly light and flavorful, the result of basing them on ground veal and milk-soaked bread and cooking them slowly and gently in the sauce.

4 tablespoons (1/2 stick) unsalted butter

1 medium onion, peeled and finely chopped

3 garlic cloves, peeled and minced

4 slices Italian bread, crusts discarded, cut into small dice

1/4 cup whole milk

2 pounds lean ground veal

1 large egg, lightly beaten

1/4 cup freshly grated Parmesan cheese

1 tablespoon chopped fresh parsley

1 tablespoon chopped fresh basil leaves

1 teaspoon chopped fresh thyme leaves

1 teaspoon salt

1 teaspoon sugar

1/4 teaspoon freshly ground black pepper

5 cups My Favorite Tomato Sauce (page 63)

1 pound dried spaghetti

Chopped fresh flat-leaf parsley, for garnish

Freshly grated Parmesan cheese, for garnish

1. In a medium skillet over medium heat, melt the butter. Add the onion and garlic and sauté until soft, about 5 minutes, taking care not to brown the onions. Remove the mixture to a small bowl and set aside to cool.

2. In a large mixing bowl, combine the bread and milk. Set aside for about 10 minutes, until all the milk is completely absorbed.

3. Add to the mixing bowl the sautéed onion

and garlic, ground veal, egg, Parmesan, parsley, basil, thyme, salt, sugar, and black pepper. With a spoon, a fork, or your hands, mix until thoroughly combined.

4. Wetting your hands with cold water, roll about one eighth of the veal mixture into a large, even meatball and place it on a large plate or baking sheet. Repeat with the remaining mixture, making 8 meatballs in all.

5. In a large saucepan over medium heat, heat the tomato sauce until it is very gently simmering. One at a time, carefully lower the meatballs into the simmering sauce. Reduce the heat and simmer very gently, covered, until the meatballs are cooked through and the sauce has thickened, about 45 minutes.

6. Bring a large pot of salted water to boil. Add the spaghetti and cook until al dente, tender but still chewy, following the manufacturer's suggested cooking time.

7. With a slotted spoon, remove the meatballs from the sauce and transfer them to a plate. Remove 1½ cups of sauce from the pan and keep it warm. Drain the spaghetti and instantly stir it into the tomato sauce in the saucepan. Toss to coat the spaghetti thoroughly. Twirl or mound the spaghetti into each of 8 warmed serving bowls or plates. Top with the meatballs and drizzle with the reserved sauce. Sprinkle with chopped parsley and Parmesan cheese, if desired.

Bucatini with Mussels, Clams, and Oven-Dried Tomatoes

SERVES 4

*N*aples is a center of dried pasta-making in Italy. Being a major fishing port, it also celebrates seafood in so many of its dishes. This particular Neapolitan favorite combines freshly harvested, quickly cooked shellfish with an intriguing form of dried pasta, bucatini, long spaghetti-like strands that have a tiny hole running through their center. You'll also sometimes see the same type of pasta referred to as perciatelli.

1 pound black mussels	2 bay leaves
1 pound littleneck clams	1 cup Oven-Dried Tomatoes (page 218)
1/4 pound (1 stick) unsalted butter	1/4 cup minced fresh flat-leaf parsley
1/4 cup minced garlic	leaves
2 cups dry white wine	Salt
3/4 pound bucatini	Freshly ground black pepper
2 cups bottled clam juice	

1. Pull from the mussels any "beards," the seaweedlike strands they use to connect to rocks or pilings. Scrub the mussels and clams thoroughly under cold running water. Soak them in a sink or basin filled with cold tap water for 5 minutes. Rinse and drain thoroughly. Repeat the soaking, rinsing, and draining 2 more times. Set the shellfish aside.

2. Bring a large pot of salted water to a boil.

3. Meanwhile, in a large sauté pan, melt the butter over medium heat. Add the garlic and cook just until it is glossy and fragrant, about 1 minute, being careful not to let it brown.

4. Pour in the white wine, raise the heat to high, and boil until it reduces by half, 5 to 7 minutes.

5. After the wine has reduced, add the bucatini to the pot of boiling water and cook until the pasta is al dente, tender but still chewy, following the manufacturer's suggested cooking time.

6. As soon as the pasta starts cooking, add to the reduced wine in the sauté pan the mussels

and clams, the clam juice, and the bay leaves. Cover and steam for 3 to 4 minutes, until the shellfish open. With a slotted spoon, remove the shellfish and reserve them in a bowl, discarding any unopened shellfish.

7. Boil the liquid in the sauté pan until it has reduced by half, 7 to 10 minutes. Add the cooked pasta, the reserved shellfish, the Oven-Dried Tomatoes, and the parsley. Toss until well blended, seasoning to taste with salt and pepper. Serve immediately.

Pumpkin Ravioli

SERVES 6

You won't believe how beautiful these ravioli look when guests cut into them and see the bright gold-orange filling, which is especially pretty in contrast with green spinach-flavored pasta dough. The slight sweetness of the pumpkin goes wonderfully with the fragrant sage and thyme used in both the filling and the

sauce. Feel free to substitute other hard-shelled winter squash varieties, such as butternut, acorn, or Hubbard. Be very careful when you cut up and peel the squash, using a good, sharp knife and always cutting away from you! Assembly and cooking take some time, but you and your guests will be very happy with the results.

1/4 pound (1 stick) plus 2 tablespoons unsalted butter	3 eggs
	Salt
1 pound fresh pumpkin, peeled, seeded, and cut into 1-inch cubes	Freshly ground white pepper
	6 sheets (each about 6 by 12 inches) fresh spinach pasta (page 209)
2 cups heavy cream	
1/2 bay leaf	1/4 cup semolina or all-purpose flour, for dusting
2 tablespoons minced fresh sage, plus 6 small whole leaves for garnish	
	2 cups Chicken Stock (page 204) or good-quality canned chicken broth
2 teaspoons minced fresh thyme leaves	2 shallots, chopped

1. Heat a large, heavy skillet over low heat and add 4 tablespoons of the butter. When the butter is foamy, add the cubed pumpkin and cook, stirring often to prevent sticking and burning, until the pumpkin is tender, 15 to 20 minutes.

2. Transfer the pumpkin to a medium saucepan. Add 1 cup of the heavy cream and half the herbs and cook over low heat, stirring and mashing the pumpkin frequently with a wooden

spoon, until it forms a thick puree with no excess liquid, about 30 minutes. If any lumps remain, use a fork to crush them into the mixture. Remove from the heat and beat in an additional 2 tablespoons butter.

3. Break 2 of the eggs into a small bowl and beat them thoroughly with a fork. Whisk the beaten eggs into the pumpkin. Season to taste with salt and pepper and set aside to cool.

4. On a floured work surface, lay out 3 sheets of pasta. Using a pastry bag or a tablespoon, place 8 equal mounds of the pumpkin puree on each sheet of dough, about 2 inches apart, using up all of the pumpkin puree. Break the remaining egg into a bowl and beat it lightly. Dip a pastry brush or your finger into the egg and use this egg wash to moisten the pasta evenly around each mound of filling. Cover each of the mounded dough sheets with a second sheet of pasta and press down around each mound of filling to seal the sheets of dough together.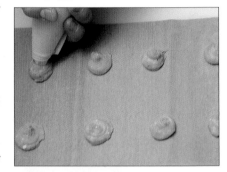

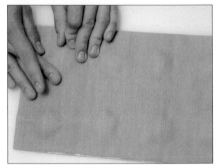

5. Dust a tray or baking sheet with the semolina. Using a 2-inch cookie cutter, cut out the ravioli, taking care to center the filling in each one and transferring each ravioli to the dusted tray as you cut it. Set the ravioli aside. Bring a large pot of salted water to a boil while you make the sauce.

6. Put the Chicken Stock and shallots in a medium saucepan. Over high heat, bring to a boil and continue boiling until the liquid has reduced to ½ cup, about 15 minutes. Stir in the remaining 1 cup heavy cream and continue boiling until the liquid reduces by half, 7 to 10 minutes. Reduce the heat to low and, a little at a time, whisk in the remaining 4 tablespoons butter. Strain the sauce into a clean saucepan, add the remaining sage and thyme, and season to taste with salt and pepper. Keep warm.

7. Add the ravioli to the rapidly boiling water and cook until al dente, 4 to 5 minutes. One by one, remove the ravioli with a slotted spoon, drain, and transfer to the sauce. Over medium heat, bring the sauce just back to a boil. Remove from the heat and adjust the seasonings to taste. Divide the ravioli among preheated plates and spoon the sauce over them. Garnish each serving with a fresh sage leaf. Serve immediately.

White Corn Agnolotti

*T*he first time guests at Spago taste these little filled pastas, they invariably close their eyes and smile and their heads begin to sway with pleasure. This absolutely original dish will repay your efforts a hundred times over when you see that look on your own guests' faces. Shavings of white truffle are the perfect, extravagant finishing touch, but the rare fungus is very expensive. If you like,

substitute a light drizzle of white truffle-infused olive oil, which you can find in small bottles in specialty foods stores.

FILLING

1 cup heavy cream

4 ears white corn, grated through the
    medium holes of a box grater
    (about 2 cups)

1 teaspoon kosher salt

1/4 teaspoon freshly ground black
    pepper

1 teaspoon sugar

1 ounce fresh, creamy goat cheese

3 ounces mascarpone cheese

2 tablespoons grated Parmesan
    cheese

1/2 teaspoon minced fresh thyme
    leaves

AGNOLOTTI

Semolina or all-purpose flour,
    for dusting

10 sheets (each about 6 by 12 inches)
    fresh pasta (page 209)

1 large egg beaten with 1 tablespoon
    water

1/2 cup Chicken Stock (page 204) or
    good-quality canned chicken broth

12 tablespoons (1 1/2 sticks) unsalted
    butter

2 sprigs of fresh sage

Salt

Freshly ground black pepper

1/4 ounce white truffle

1. To make the filling: In a medium skillet over medium-high heat, bring the cream to a boil. Continue boiling until it has reduced to ⅓ cup, about 10 minutes. Stir in the grated corn, salt, pepper, and sugar. Stirring constantly, bring the mixture back to a slow boil. Reduce the heat slightly and continue to cook, stirring frequently, until the mixture reduces and is thick enough to heavily coat the back of the spoon.

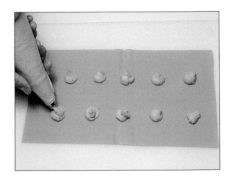

2. Transfer the mixture to a medium bowl. Stir in the goat cheese, mascarpone, Parmesan, and thyme until the cheese has melted and thoroughly blended in. Taste and adjust the seasonings with salt and pepper. Place the bowl inside a larger bowl filled with ice and stir occasionally until the filling has cooled and set.

3. To make the agnolotti: Use a flour-dusted rolling pin to roll out the pasta sheets on a lightly floured board as thin as possible. With a pastry bag or a teaspoon, mound little heaps of the filling about 1 inch apart in 2 parallel rows. Dip a pastry brush or your finger into the beaten egg and use it to moisten the pasta completely around each mound of filling. Cut the pasta sheet lengthwise in half between the rows. Fold each strip of dough in half lengthwise over the mounds of filling and press down and pinch the dough with your fingers to seal the dough firmly around each mound. With a serrated pastry wheel, cut the pasta between each mound; then, use it to trim away excess dough from each of the agnolotti, leaving no more than about ¼ inch on each sealed side. Pinch the edges to seal the agnolotti firmly.

4. Bring a large pot of salted water to a boil. Meanwhile, in a heavy skillet, combine the Chicken Stock, butter, and sage; bring to a boil over high heat and continue boiling and gently swirling the pan until the mixture forms a smooth, thick emulsion. Season to taste with salt and pepper and keep warm.

5. Cook the agnolotti in the boiling water until al dente, 2 to 3 minutes. Remove with a slotted spoon, drain, and add to the sage-butter sauce. Transfer the agnolotti and their sauce to warmed soup plates or bowls and thinly shave the white truffle over them. To capture the truffle aroma released by the pasta's heat, cover each serving with another plate. At the table, instruct guests to lift off their top plates and enjoy the burst of truffle aroma before they eat the agnolotti.

Wild Mushroom Risotto

*M*aking risotto requires your full attention and a lot of stirring. The stirring helps dissolve the generous surface starch of the short-grained rice varieties used for the dish, producing risotto's signature creamy sauce. Risotto has become so popular that you'll probably find at least one of the three most common rice varieties used for it—Arborio, carnaroli, and vialone nano—in Italian markets and in the grains or specialty-foods aisles of most well-stocked supermarkets. The rice can be partially cooked in advance through step 3 below and then cooled. But the final cooking and finishing process is so precise that the risotto cannot wait for your guests; rather, your guests have to wait for the risotto. Many people still refer to the mushroom varieties I call for here as wild even though they are all cultivated commercially.

7 cups Chicken Stock (page 204) or good-quality canned chicken broth

$1/2$ pound wild mushrooms such as shiitake, cremini, oyster, or portobello, stems trimmed off and reserved for stock, caps cut into bite-size pieces if necessary

$1/3$ cup peanut oil

1 large onion, peeled and chopped

1 large garlic clove, peeled and minced

2 cups Arborio, carnaroli, or vialone nano rice

1 cup dry white wine

3 tablespoons extra-virgin olive oil

1 medium tomato, peeled, seeded, and chopped (page 217)

4 tablespoons ($1/2$ stick) unsalted butter, chilled and cut into small pieces

$1/2$ cup grated Parmesan cheese

1 tablespoon chopped flat-leaf parsley

Salt

Freshly ground black pepper

1. Put the stock in a saucepan and add the mushroom stems. Bring the stock to a boil. Reduce the heat to maintain a bare simmer.

2. In a heavy, medium saucepan, heat the peanut oil over medium-high heat. Add the onion and garlic and sauté, stirring constantly with a wooden spoon, just until softened, 3 to 4 minutes. Add the rice and continue to stir for 1 to 2 minutes more, until the rice is thoroughly coated with the oil.

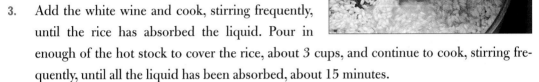

3. Add the white wine and cook, stirring frequently, until the rice has absorbed the liquid. Pour in enough of the hot stock to cover the rice, about 3 cups, and continue to cook, stirring frequently, until all the liquid has been absorbed, about 15 minutes.

4. Meanwhile, in a medium skillet, heat the olive oil over medium-high heat. Add the mushrooms and sauté just until the mushrooms have softened, 3 to 4 minutes.

5. Pour 3 more cups of the hot stock into the rice, raise the heat to high, and stir in the tomato. Continue to cook, stirring frequently, until the rice is almost al dente, tender but still fairly chewy, about 15 minutes more. Stir in the mushrooms. Stir in enough of the remaining 1 cup of stock to make the risotto creamy but not runny.

6. Remove the risotto from the heat and, with the wooden spoon, vigorously beat in the chilled butter and ¼ cup of the Parmesan cheese until completely incorporated. Stir in the parsley and season with salt and pepper to taste. Divide the risotto among 4 heated plates or shallow serving bowls and serve immediately, passing the remaining ¼ cup Parmesan cheese for guests to add as desired.

SEAFOOD

Spicy Shrimp Tempura with Cilantro

Crispy Shrimp with Chinese Noodles and Spicy Garlic Sauce

Grilled Shrimp with Ginger and Lime

Lobster with Sweet Ginger

Lobster Imperial in Black Bean Sauce

Seared Tuna au Poivre

Acqua Pazza with Sea Bass, Clams, and Mussels

Pan-Seared Sea Bass with Cannellini Beans, Braised Escarole,
    and Cherry Tomato Vinaigrette

Sea Bass with Lemon and Caper Sauce

Roasted Black Bass on Jasmine Rice with Miso Glaze

Marinated and Glazed Swordfish

Spicy Shrimp Tempura with Cilantro

SERVES 4

*L*ots of people first fall in love with Japanese cooking through tempura, that culture's technique for deep-frying foods with an incomparably light, crisp batter. But you might be surprised to learn that tempura is not really Japanese in origin. They learned both the technique and the word in the sixteenth century from Portuguese and Spanish traders, who ate fried seafood during Lent, one of four annual fasting periods referred to in Latin as *Quattor Tempora*. Of course, Japanese cooks greatly refined the Mediterranean approach, using a thin, ice-cold batter and fresh, perfectly heated oil. I've spiced up the recipe with hot peppers and fresh cilantro, which brings it back a little bit to its Hispanic roots. If you like, serve the shrimp with some Cilantro-Mint Vinaigrette (page 150), shown in the photo here.

12 jumbo shrimp

1 large or 2 small jalapeño chilies, seeded and finely chopped

2 tablespoons chopped fresh cilantro leaves

Juice of 2 medium limes

Salt

TEMPURA BATTER

1 cup all-purpose flour

1 tablespoon baking powder

1¹/4 cups water

2 tablespoons sesame seeds

¹/2 teaspoon cayenne pepper

¹/4 cup finely chopped cilantro leaves

Salt

Peanut oil for frying

1 bunch of spinach, leaves only, trimmed, thoroughly washed and dried

1. Peel the shrimp. With a small, sharp knife, devein them by cutting a shallow slit along their backs, the outer curve, and removing the threadlike digestive tract. Butterfly the shrimp by

cutting deeper along their backs, about halfway through, to open them into two attached lobes. Place the shrimp in a single layer on a large platter. Sprinkle them with the chopped jalapeño and chopped cilantro. Sprinkle the lime juice over them, cover with plastic wrap, and marinate in the refrigerator for at least 30 minutes and no more than a few hours. When ready to cook, season the shrimp lightly with salt.

2. Before cooking, prepare the batter: In a small mixing bowl, sift together the flour and baking powder. Whisk in the water until a smooth batter has formed, then stir in the sesame seeds, cayenne pepper, chopped cilantro, and salt to taste. Nestle the bowl of batter inside a larger bowl filled with ice, to keep the batter cold and ensure crisp results.

3. At serving time, in a deep, heavy saucepan, wok, or deep-fryer, heat 3 inches of oil to 350°F. Preheat the oven to its lowest setting.

4. Working with 3 or 4 shrimps at a time, dip each one in the batter to coat it well, and then carefully drop it into the hot oil, taking care to avoid splashing or splattering. Fry the shrimp until golden brown, about 2 minutes. With metal tongs, a slotted spoon, or wire skimmer, remove the shrimp from the oil and transfer to paper towels to drain. Transfer the shrimp to a heatproof dish and keep them warm in the low oven while preparing the remaining shrimp.

5. In the same oil, deep-fry the spinach, using the slotted spoon or skimmer to keep the leaves submerged until crisp and translucent, 1 to 2 minutes. Remove them with the slotted spoon or skimmer, drain on paper towels, and season lightly with salt.

6. Arrange a bed of fried spinach leaves on each of 4 plates. Place 3 shrimp on top of or next to the spinach and serve immediately.

Crispy Shrimp with Chinese Noodles and Spicy Garlic Sauce

SERVES 4

*P*lease don't be scared off by the length of this recipe, which is based on a favorite dish featuring squid that we serve at my Asian restaurant, **Chinois on Main**. It's really very easy. You can make the sauce ahead of time. Then, when you're ready to eat, all you have to do is cook the noodles and fry the shrimp. You'll find the rice wine and rice vinegar, the soy and chili sauces, and the **C**hinese egg noodles in Asian markets or well-stocked supermarkets.

Oil for deep-frying

SAUCE
2 tablespoons peanut oil
3/4 cup sliced Double-Blanched
    Garlic, 4 ounces (page 220)
2 tablespoons sugar
1 cup rice wine
1/4 cup rice wine vinegar
2 tablespoons plus 1 teaspoon dark
    soy sauce
1 cup peeled, trimmed, and julienned
    carrots

1 cup trimmed haricots verts (before
    trimming: blanch for 1 minute in
    boiling water, refresh under cold
    running water, and dry)
1 cup trimmed green onion strips
2 teaspoons Vietnamese chili sauce

Kosher salt
12 ounces fresh thin Chinese egg
    noodles or thin spaghetti
1 pound large shrimp, peeled and
    deveined, tail fins removed
Freshly ground black pepper
About 1/2 cup all-purpose flour
1/4 teaspoon Asian toasted
    sesame oil

1. Bring a large stockpot of water to a boil. In a wok or deep, heavy saucepan, heat about 3 inches of peanut oil or vegetable oil over high heat to 375°F on a deep-frying thermometer.

2. Meanwhile, make the sauce: In a large skillet or sauté pan, heat the 2 tablespoons of peanut oil over medium-high heat. Sauté the garlic just until golden, 2 to 3 minutes. Stir in

the sugar and continue to sauté, stirring continuously, until the garlic begins to caramelize, 1 to 2 minutes longer. Add the rice wine, rice wine vinegar, and soy sauce and stir and scrape to deglaze the pan. Add the carrots, haricots verts, and about ¾ cup of the green onion, reserving the remainder for a garnish. Stir in the chili sauce and continue to cook until the sauce has reduced by half, about 5 minutes.

3. While the sauce reduces, add salt to the boiling water and cook the noodles until they are al dente, tender but still chewy. (Fresh store-bought Chinese egg noodles should take 2 to 3 minutes; for thin spaghetti, follow the manufacturer's suggested cooking time.) Drain the noodles well and stir them into the sauce until they are well coated.

4. Season the shrimp with salt and pepper and toss with the flour to coat them lightly. Deep-fry the shrimp in small batches until golden, 1 to 2 minutes. (The easiest way to do this is to use a fine-mesh basket or strainer. Place the shrimp in the basket and gently ease the basket into the oil.) Drain on paper towels.

5. To serve, divide the noodles and sauce among 4 large warmed plates. Arrange the shrimp over and around each portion and garnish with the remaining green onions. Drizzle the sesame oil over the noodles and serve immediately.

Grilled Shrimp with Ginger and Lime

Fresh limes and fresh ginger give this very fast and easy dish a real spark of flavor. While the shrimp are ideal for cooking outdoors on a lazy summer day, you'll also get great results at any time of year indoors with a broiler. Serve as a light main course with rice or grilled vegetables, or as an appetizer atop a bed of mixed greens.

MARINADE

3 tablespoons fresh lime juice

3 tablespoons extra-virgin olive oil

1 tablespoon minced ginger

1 tablespoon brown sugar

1 teaspoon grated lime zest

1 teaspoon Asian toasted sesame oil

1 large garlic clove, peeled and minced

1 pound large shrimp, peeled and deveined

2 limes, each cut into 4 wedges

2 tablespoons chopped fresh cilantro

1. In a large bowl, whisk together the lime juice, olive oil, ginger, brown sugar, lime zest, sesame oil, and garlic. Add the shrimp to this marinade and toss to coat them thoroughly. Cover the bowl with plastic wrap and refrigerate for 1 to 3 hours.

2. Preheat the grill or broiler. Thread the shrimp and the lime wedges onto 8 skewers, dividing them evenly and alternating them.

3. Cook the shrimp skewers on the grill directly over the heat, or 3 to 4 inches under the broiler, until they are uniformly bright pink, about 5 minutes total cooking time, turning them once halfway through. Serve immediately, sprinkled with cilantro.

Lobster with Sweet Ginger

*L*ook like a superstar in the kitchen with this dramatic, dynamically flavored classic from **Chinois** on **Main.** I've known guests who won't let the serving platter leave the table until they've spooned up every last drop of the sauce. The recipe can be doubled fairly easily, but you'll need a larger skillet, or a second one, to cook the second lobster, and you'll have to

allow a few more minutes for reducing the sauce to the right consistency. You'll find the plum wine and rice vinegar in a **Chinese** market or the **Asian** foods section of a well-stocked supermarket.

1 live lobster, 2 pounds	1/2 cup Fish Stock (page 206)
1-inch piece fresh ginger	1/4 cup dry white wine
2 garlic cloves, peeled and minced	1 tablespoon Chinese black vinegar or
3/4 cup plum wine or port	balsamic vinegar
2 tablespoons rice vinegar	1/2 teaspoon chili flakes
2 tablespoons peanut oil	1/2 cup heavy cream
2 tablespoons unsalted butter	Salt
4 scallions, cut into 3/8-inch slices	Freshly ground black pepper
1 to 2 teaspoons curry powder	Fried Spinach Leaves (page 159)

1. Preheat the oven to 500°F. If you're hesitant about splitting the lobster in half while it's still alive, first plunge it into a large pot of boiling water and parboil it for only about half a minute; then drain immediately and rinse with cold running water until cool. With a large, sharp, sturdy chef's knife, carefully split the live or parboiled lobster in half lengthwise. To do this, place it on a cutting board on its back, holding its tail down with a kitchen towel and keeping clear of its claws; pierce it with the knife tip midway between its first and second pairs of legs, then cut down through its head; and turn it around and cut down

through the tail to produce two symmetrical halves. To clean the lobster, pull out the sand sac near its head. With the knife tip, lift out and discard the gray intestinal vein running through its back. Set the lobster aside.

2. Peel the ginger, reserving the peels, and cut the ginger into fine julienne strips, setting them aside. Cut the peels into coarse strips and set them aside as well.

3. In a small saucepan over medium-high heat, cook the julienned ginger and garlic with ½ cup of the plum wine and the rice vinegar until 1 tablespoon of liquid remains, about 5 minutes. Remove from the heat and set aside.

4. Place a heavy, ovenproof 12-inch skillet over high heat until it is very hot. Add the oil and heat it almost to the smoking point. Carefully add the lobster halves, meat side down. Cook for 3 minutes. Turn the lobster over and add 1 tablespoon of butter to the skillet. Continue to sauté the lobster shells until they are red and the butter is a nutty red color, about 2 minutes more. Transfer the skillet to the oven and continue cooking until the lobster meat is just cooked through, about 10 minutes. Remove the skillet from the oven. Using tongs, transfer the lobster halves to a covered, heatproof dish and keep them warm.

5. Put the skillet over medium-high heat, add the scallions, ginger peels, and curry powder, and sauté the mixture lightly for 15 seconds, until fragrant, then whisk in the remaining plum wine and the stock, white wine, vinegar, and chili flakes. Boil until the liquid has reduced to about ½ cup, 10 to 15 minutes. Add the cream and reduce by half, 5 to 7 minutes, then whisk in the remaining 1 tablespoon of butter. Season the sauce to taste with salt and pepper.

6. Crack the lobster claws with the back of the chef's knife. Arrange the lobster halves on a warmed oval platter, meat side up. Hold a fine-meshed strainer over the platter and pour the sauce through it over the lobster. Sprinkle the sweet ginger julienne on top. Garnish with fried spinach leaves.

Lobster Imperial in Black Bean Sauce

SERVES 1 OR 2

*S*ome of my favorite Asian cuisines come together in this delicious and easy lobster dish, perfect for a special dinner for two or a gala meal accompanied by other dishes from the **Far East.** The fermented black beans are **Chinese,** and you can probably guess where the **Japanese** leeks come from. You may have to search in ethnic markets for the slender leeks, which look like over-grown scallions; or just substitute the biggest scallion you can find or two or three smaller ones. **Chinese** black beans may be found in **Asian** markets or well-stocked supermarkets.

1 live lobster, 1¹/₂-pounds

Salt

Freshly ground black pepper

Potato starch, for coating

Peanut oil, for deep-frying and stir-frying

¹/₄ cup Chicken Stock (page 204) or good-quality canned broth, cold or at room temperature

¹/₂ teaspoon cornstarch

1 tablespoon fermented black beans, chopped

1 tablespoon minced garlic

1 tablespoon sugar

1 head baby bok choy, trimmed and cut into 1-inch chunks

1 Japanese or wild leek, cut into thin diagonal slices

2 ounces snow peas, trimmed, each cut diagonally in half

1. If you're hesitant about splitting the lobster in half while it's still alive, first plunge it into a large pot of boiling water and parboil it for only about half a minute; then drain immediately and rinse with cold running water until cool. With a large, sharp, sturdy chef's knife, carefully split the live or parboiled lobster in half lengthwise. To do this, place it on a cutting board on its back, holding its tail down with a kitchen towel and keeping clear of its claws; pierce it with the knife tip midway between its first and second pairs of legs, then cut down through its head; and turn it around and cut down through the tail to produce two symmetrical halves. To clean the lobster, pull out the sand sac near its head. With the knife tip, lift out and discard the gray intestinal vein running through its back. Set the lobster aside. Cut off the claws and split them in half lengthwise. Cut the rest of the lobster halves in large chunks.

2. Place all the lobster pieces in a large mixing bowl and season with salt and pepper to taste. Sprinkle on enough potato starch to coat all the pieces lightly and evenly.

3. Fill a deep-fryer, wok, or large, deep, heavy skillet with several inches of peanut oil. Over high heat, heat the oil to 400°F on a deep-frying thermometer. Shaking off any excess potato starch into the bowl, carefully add the lobster pieces to the hot oil. Deep-fry them until the shells have turned bright red and the meat is cooked through, 1½ to 2 minutes. With a wire skimmer or slotted spoon, remove the lobster pieces from the oil and drain on paper towels.

4. In a small bowl or cup, stir together the stock and cornstarch until the cornstarch has completely dissolved, with no lumps remaining. Heat a clean wok over high heat. Add 2 tablespoons of fresh peanut oil and the black beans, garlic, and sugar, and stir-fry for 10 seconds. Add the bok choy, leek, and snow peas and continue to stir-fry for another 10 seconds. Add the stock-cornstarch mixture and stir and scrape to dissolve any pan deposits; immediately add all the lobster pieces and continue to stir-fry for 20 seconds more, turning the lobster in the sauce to coat it well. Transfer the lobster, vegetables, and sauce to a heated plate or platter and arrange the lobster pieces decoratively. Serve immediately.

Seared Tuna au Poivre

*T*he first rule for making a great fish dish is always to buy the freshest fish. For this recipe, which treats tuna to the crushed-pepper coating traditionally used for steak in French cuisine, I buy sushi-grade ahi, which is a deep red color and almost as rich and meaty-tasting as prime beef. For the most appealing presentation, I cut away the darker blood line from the fillets. Searing the steaks for less than a minute per side to cook them rare ensures that the tuna stays moist and flavorful, like a great steak. A sauce of port and cognac makes a fitting accompaniment, and you might even want to serve mashed potatoes alongside.

4 tuna steaks, 6 ounces each

Salt

1/4 cup cracked black peppercorns

1/3 cup port

1/4 cup cognac

1/2 cup reduced **Brown Chicken Stock**
    (page 205) or reduced good-quality
    canned broth

2 tablespoons unsalted butter,
    cut into pieces

Freshly ground black pepper

2 teaspoons bottled green
    peppercorns, drained

1. Season the tuna steaks lightly with salt. Pour the peppercorns on a sheet of waxed paper or a large plate and press each piece of tuna into the pepper to coat both sides evenly. Place on a plate, cover with plastic wrap, and refrigerate until needed.

2. Put the port and cognac in a small skillet or saucepan and boil over medium-high heat until 2 tablespoons remain, 7 to 10 minutes. Stir in the stock and continue boiling a few minutes

more until the sauce reduces and thickens. Pour the sauce through a strainer into a clean pan, whisk in the butter, and season to taste with a little salt and black pepper. Cover the pan and keep warm.

3. Select a skillet large enough to hold the 4 tuna steaks in one layer and preheat it over high heat. In the skillet, sear the tuna until its surface is nicely browned and firm, 35 to 45 seconds per side. Cut each steak crosswise into ½-inch-thick slices. Spoon a little sauce in the center of each of 4 plates. Arrange the seared tuna slices on top of the sauce and garnish with the green peppercorns. Serve immediately.

Acqua Pazza with Sea Bass, Clams, and Mussels

SERVES 4

"**C**razy water" is what the **Neapolitans** call this wild mixture of fish, shellfish, and vegetables, all joined together by a tomato sauce spiced with garlic, hot pepper, and fragrant saffron. One taste and you can see its relationship to the classic bouillabaisse of France, although this recipe is definitely, passionately Italian. The recipe will take up most of the burners on your stove, requiring three separate skillets, but it comes together very quickly and easily, so have all the ingredients prepared and ready to go before you start cooking. You could substitute other firm, white-fleshed fish for the sea bass, and add some large shrimp in place of some of the shellfish if you like. I love to eat this kind of dish on a chilly winter evening; its flavors are so warming.

8 tablespoons extra-virgin olive oil	2 Italian eggplants, ends trimmed, thinly sliced
1 large onion, peeled and thinly sliced	1 green zucchini, ends trimmed, thinly sliced
1 tablespoon minced garlic	
2 cups Tomato Concassé (page 217)	1 yellow zucchini, ends trimmed, thinly sliced
$^{1}/_{4}$ teaspoon cayenne pepper	
Generous pinch of saffron threads	10 basil leaves, cut crosswise into chiffonade strips (page 229)
1 pound littleneck clams, thoroughly rinsed and scrubbed	4 sea bass fillets, 6 ounces each
1 pound black mussels, debearded, thoroughly rinsed and scrubbed	1 tablespoon unsalted butter
	1 red bell pepper, stemmed, seeded, and cut into $^{1}/_{4}$-inch dice
$^{1}/_{2}$ cup dry white wine	
Salt	4 tablespoons Basil Oil (page 224)
Freshly ground black pepper	

1. Preheat the oven to 350°F.

2. In a sauté pan over medium heat, warm 2 tablespoons of the olive oil. Add the onion and garlic and sauté until they are soft, glossy, and just beginning to brown, 5 to 7 minutes. Add the tomatoes, cayenne, and saffron, and cook for 5 minutes more. Add the clams, mussels, and white wine. Cover and continue to cook for another 3 minutes. Remove the pan

from the heat. Taste and adjust the seasoning with salt and pepper. Set the pan aside and keep warm.

3. In another sauté pan over high heat, add 3 tablespoons of olive oil. Add the eggplant slices and sauté until lightly browned, about 5 minutes. Add the green and yellow zucchini and sauté 1 minute more, just until they are heated. Add 1 tablespoon of the basil chiffonade. Season to taste with salt and pepper. Set the pan aside.

4. Season the sea bass fillets with salt and pepper. In a third, ovenproof sauté pan, heat the remaining 3 tablespoons of olive oil over medium-high heat. Sear the fillets until their undersides are golden, about 2 minutes. Transfer the pan to the preheated oven and continue to cook another 4 minutes. Transfer the pan back to the burner, turn the fillets, and reduce the heat to medium. Add the butter and, as it melts, baste the fillets with the butter-oil mixture. Continue cooking just until the fish is cooked through and flakes when a fillet is pierced with the tip of a small, sharp knife, 3 to 4 minutes more.

5. To serve, distribute the tomato sauce and shellfish evenly among 4 heated serving plates or large, shallow soup bowls, discarding any unopened shellfish. Spoon the sautéed vegetables into the center of each plate and top with a sea bass fillet. Garnish with the diced bell pepper and remaining chiffonade of basil. Drizzle the Basil Oil around the edge of the tomato sauce on each plate and serve immediately.

Pan-Seared Sea Bass with Cannellini Beans, Braised Escarole, and Cherry Tomato Vinaigrette

SERVES 6

*I*f you want to spend a weekend afternoon preparing something that will impress just about anyone, try this rustic Italian-style dish. The recipe might seem complicated at first, but each separate procedure in it is actually very simple. You'll have a good time—and you and your guests will enjoy a great meal.

WHITE BEAN RAGOUT

1 pound dry cannellini beans, soaked in water overnight

1/2 pound pancetta, cut into large chunks

1/4 cup extra-virgin olive oil

2 large carrots, cut into 1/4-inch dice

2 stalks celery, cut into 1/4-inch dice

1 large red onion, peeled and cut into 1/4-inch dice

1/4 cup chopped garlic

3 tablespoons tomato paste

2 cups Chicken Stock (page 204) or good-quality canned chicken broth

1 tablespoon salt

1 teaspoon freshly ground black pepper

2 bunches of spinach, thoroughly washed and stemmed

CHERRY TOMATO VINAIGRETTE

1/2 cup extra-virgin olive oil

2 tablespoons balsamic vinegar

2 tablespoons lemon juice

1 teaspoon kosher salt

1/2 teaspoon freshly ground black pepper

1 pint ripe cherry tomatoes, stemmed and cut into quarters

¹⁄₄ cup oil-packed sun-dried
   tomatoes, chopped
6 large basil leaves, cut crosswise
   into chiffonade strips (page 229)

SEA BASS
6 eight-ounce or 12 four-ounce sea
   bass fillets, skin left on, scaled
3 tablespoons extra-virgin olive oil
Kosher salt
Finely ground white pepper

ESCAROLE
2 tablespoons extra-virgin olive oil
2 heads escarole, outer leaves
   trimmed, each head cut into 6
   wedges

1. First, prepare the White Bean Ragout: Discard the soaking water from the cannellini beans. In a large saucepan over medium-high heat, sauté the pancetta until it begins to render some of its fat and turns golden, about 5 minutes. Add the drained cannellini beans and 5 cups of cold water. Raise the heat to high and bring the water to a boil; reduce the heat to maintain a simmer and  cook the beans until tender but still firm, about 45 minutes. Place a strainer over a heat-proof mixing bowl. Strain the beans, reserving the cooking liquid in the bowl; discard the pancetta chunks. Set the beans and liquid aside.

2. In a large saucepan over medium-high heat, heat the olive oil. Add the carrots, celery, red onion, and garlic and sauté until the onion is transparent, about 8 minutes.

3. In a small bowl, blend the tomato paste with ½ cup of cold water. Add the diluted tomato paste to the sautéed vegetables along with the reserved cannellini beans, their cooking liquid, and the Chicken Stock. Season with salt and black pepper. Bring to a boil; reduce the heat and simmer, covered, until the beans are very tender and the mixture has reduced by about one fourth. Stir in the spinach and cook until it has wilted, about 3 minutes more. Set aside and keep warm.

4. Next, prepare the Cherry Tomato Vinaigrette: In a large bowl, whisk together the olive oil, balsamic vinegar, lemon juice, salt, and black pepper. Stir in the cherry tomatoes, sun-dried tomatoes, and basil chiffonade. Set aside.

5. Prepare the sea bass: Preheat the oven to 400°F. Brush the sea bass fillets all over with 1 tablespoon of the olive oil. With a sharp knife, score a crisscross pattern on the skin side of the fillets to help keep them from curling as they cook. Season the fillets with salt and white pepper. In a large, heavy, ovenproof skillet over high heat, heat the remaining 2 tablespoons of olive oil. Add the sea bass, skin side down, and sauté for 2 minutes. Transfer the pan to the preheated oven and bake until the fish flakes when the tip of a small, sharp knife is inserted into the center of one fillet, 5 to 6 minutes more. To ensure a crisp skin, do not turn the fish.

6. While the fish is in the oven, prepare the escarole: In a clean, large skillet over medium heat, heat the olive oil. Sauté the escarole until it has wilted, about 5 minutes.

7. To serve, ladle the White Bean Ragout into 6 large, heated soup plates. Arrange two wedges of escarole overlapping on top of the beans. With a metal spatula, carefully place one large or two small sea bass fillets on top of the escarole in each plate. Spoon the Cherry Tomato Vinaigrette over the sea bass. Serve immediately.

Sea Bass with Lemon and Caper Sauce

SERVES 4

*L*emon, capers, and butter combine to make one of the simplest, most classic Mediterranean treatments for sautéed fish. Sea bass is a perfect choice, but any firm white fish fillets may be substituted. Assorted baby vegetables, blanched in boiling water for 2 minutes and then sautéed in butter until al dente and glazed, make a pretty accompaniment, alongside or mounded beneath the fish. Crunchy, buttery croutons add just the right finishing touch to this delicate dish.

2 lemons

12 tablespoons (1½ sticks) unsalted butter

2 or 3 slices fresh white bread, brioche, or baguette, crusts trimmed and discarded, crumb cut into ½-inch cubes, about 1 cup total

4 sea bass fillets, 6 ounces each, skin left on, scaled

Salt

Freshly ground white pepper

4 tablespoons extra-virgin olive oil

1 small red bell pepper, stemmed, seeded, and cut into small dice

2 tablespoons minced shallots

¼ cup minced fresh parsley leaves

¼ cup minced fresh chives

2 teaspoons minced fresh tarragon leaves

2 tablespoons capers, drained and rinsed

2 tablespoons caper berries, drained and cut lengthwise in halves

1. Preheat the oven to 350°F.

2. Meanwhile, prepare the lemons: Holding a lemon on its end, use a sharp knife to cut down along the peel, removing it in strips thick enough to expose the pulp of its segments beneath the white pith and membrane. When all the peel has been removed, working over a bowl to catch the juices, use the knife to cut carefully between the membrane and pulp of each segment, freeing the segment and letting it drop into the bowl. Squeeze any remaining juice from the pulp left clinging to the membranes and discard the membranes and peels. Repeat with the other lemon. Coarsely chop the segments, discarding the seeds. Measure out ½ cup of segments and juice and set aside, reserving any remaining for another use.

3. To make croutons, melt 4 tablespoons of the butter in a small saucepan over low heat or in a glass bowl in the microwave. Toss the bread cubes with the butter and spread them on a small baking sheet or in a baking dish. Put them in the oven and bake until crisp and golden, 5 to 7 minutes. Transfer to a bowl and set aside.

4. Season the sea bass fillets with salt and pepper. With a sharp knife, score a crisscross pattern on the skin side of the fillets to keep them from curling as they cook. In a sauté pan over high heat, heat the olive oil. Add the sea bass fillets skin side down and sear them until golden brown, about 3 minutes. With a metal spatula, turn the fillets over and cook until the fish flakes when a knife tip is inserted in the center of one, about 4 minutes more.

5. Add the remaining 8 tablespoons of butter to the fillets and baste them as it melts. Place a fillet on each of 4 heated serving plates and garnish with the red bell pepper dice. Sprinkle the croutons evenly over and around each fillet. To the butter in the skillet, add the shallots and continue to sauté them over high heat until the butter turns brown. Strain in the lemon juice and stir and scrape with a wooden spoon to deglaze the pan deposits; add the lemon pieces, parsley, chives, tarragon, capers, and caper berries. When the ingredients are heated through, after about 1 minute, spoon the mixture over and around each fillet. Serve immediately.

Roasted Black Bass on Jasmine Rice with Miso Glaze

SERVES 4

*B*lack bass has firm, mild white meat that goes wonderfully with traditional seasonings of Japan. Feel free to substitute any other firm white fish fillets. You'll find all the Asian ingredients you need in most well-stocked supermarkets today. Use yellow miso, also known by the Japanese as *shinshu-miso,* if you can't find white or *shiro* miso; both kinds will be in airtight containers in the refrigerated case. Jasmine rice, a Thai specialty now widely grown, has a delicate fragrance reminiscent of that flower. The portions are on the small side, assuming you're serving the fish Asian-style with an assortment of other dishes. Allow 5 to 6 hours to marinate the fish.

1/4 cup white miso paste	1 teaspoon minced fresh ginger
1/2 cup mirin (Japanese sweet cooking wine) or good-quality sweet sherry	1 tablespoon Asian toasted sesame oil
2 tablespoons sugar	4 black bass fillets, 3 ounces each
1 tablespoon mushroom soy sauce	1 cup jasmine rice
1 teaspoon minced garlic	1¼ cups water
	4 iceberg lettuce leaves

1. In a small bowl, stir together the miso, mirin, sugar, soy sauce, garlic, and ginger until the miso has dissolved. Stirring briskly, drizzle in the sesame oil to complete the miso glaze.

2. Put the bass fillets in a single layer in a shallow nonreactive dish. Spoon the miso glaze over the fillets and turn them in it to coat them evenly. Cover and refrigerate for 5 to 6 hours.

3. Preheat the oven to 500°F.

4. In a heavy saucepan, combine the rice and water. Over high heat, bring the liquid to a boil. Reduce the heat to very low, cover the pan, and cook for 15 minutes. Leave the pan covered, remove it from the heat, and let it stand for 10 minutes more.

5. While the rice is standing, arrange the fish fillets in a small roasting pan and generously spoon over them the miso glaze. Bake until done medium, cooked through but still tender and juicy when the center is pierced with the tip of a small, sharp knife, 8 to 10 minutes.

6. Place an iceberg lettuce leaf to form a cup on each of 4 serving plates. Spoon the jasmine rice into the lettuce cups. Place a black bass fillet on top of each cup of rice. Spoon the miso glaze from the roasting pan over the fish and rice.

Marinated and Glazed Swordfish

Hearty swordfish fillets make a robust, satisfying grilled main course, even for devoted meat lovers. The spicy sweet-and-sour glaze turns a quickly prepared recipe into something special for your guests. To add a pleasant nutty flavor, substitute hazelnut oil for the extra-virgin olive oil you use in the glaze. Serve the swordfish with mixed baby greens for a light summer main course; with jasmine rice, cooked following the method in the recipe on page 101; or with your favorite vegetable. Or serve each fillet in a fresh-baked split bakery bun or roll that you've brushed with olive oil and toasted lightly on the grill.

4 one-inch-thick swordfish fillets,
    about 6 ounces each
6 tablespoons extra-virgin olive oil,
    plus extra for grilling
Freshly ground black pepper
1/4 cup fresh orange juice
1/4 cup fresh lemon juice
1/4 cup white wine vinegar

2 tablespoons orange or tangerine
    marmalade
1 teaspoon minced fresh ginger
1 teaspoon minced garlic
1/2 teaspoon freshly ground white
    pepper
Salt

1. With a sharp knife, trim any skin from the side of each swordfish fillet. Put the swordfish fillets in a dish large enough to hold them side by side. Brush them all over with 2 tablespoons of the olive oil. Grind a little black pepper over both sides of the fillets. Cover the dish with plastic wrap and refrigerate until ready to cook.

2. In a nonreactive saucepan, stir together the orange juice, lemon juice, vinegar, marmalade, ginger, garlic, and white pepper. Over medium-high heat, bring the mixture to a boil; reduce the heat slightly and continue boiling until the mixture reduces to about ½ cup, 5 to 7 minutes. Remove the pan from the heat and let the mixture cool. Whisk in the remaining ¼ cup of olive oil. Transfer to a nonreactive dish, cover with plastic wrap, and refrigerate until ready to use.

3. Build a fire in a charcoal grill or preheat an outdoor or indoor gas or electric grill.

4. Return the marinade to a small saucepan and, over low heat, warm it up.

5. Brush the swordfish fillets all over with the marinade and season them lightly with salt. Brush the grill's cooking surface with some extra-virgin olive oil to prevent the fish from sticking. Grill the swordfish fillets until they are nicely browned and feel springy to the touch, 4 to 5 minutes per side. Transfer to warmed serving plates and serve immediately.

Pan-Roasted Chicken Breasts Stuffed with Bell Peppers
with Sweet Green Onion Sauce

Grilled Chicken Breasts with Garlic and Parsley

Grilled Italian Chicken with Summer Squash

Grilled Chicken Kebabs with Lemon and Thyme

Barbecued Butterflied Chicken with
Orange-Sherry Marinade

My Mother's Chicken-Stuffed Bell Peppers with
Tomato Sauce

All-American Chicken Pot Pie

Wiener Backhendl

Turkey Mushroom Burgers with Chunky Tomato
Salsa Compote

Pan-Roasted Chicken Breasts Stuffed with Bell Peppers with Sweet Green Onion Sauce

SERVES 4

*T*he extra effort it takes to flatten, stuff, and roll these chicken breasts pays off in beautiful, delicious results. Many people today don't even want to think about cooking chicken pieces with the skin on. But I leave the skin on in this recipe for good reasons. It gives the finished dish a lovely golden-brown color that you couldn't achieve otherwise. More important, though, is the fact that the skin helps seal in the chicken's moisture and flavor during pan roasting, making the results incredibly juicy. You and your guests can always leave the crisp skin behind on your plates. But you just might find it irresistible.

4 large chicken breast halves, boneless, skin on	1 tablespoon extra-virgin olive oil
Salt	3 tablespoons rice wine vinegar
Freshly ground white pepper	4 tablespoons plum wine or sherry
1 red bell pepper	1/2 cup heavy cream
1 yellow bell pepper	4 tablespoons (1/2 stick) unsalted butter, at room temperature
2 bunches scallions, ends trimmed	Chopped fresh chives, for garnish

1. With a meat pounder or a rolling pin, pound the chicken breasts between sheets of heavy-duty plastic wrap until they have a uniform thickness of about ¼ inch. Season them on both sides with salt and white pepper.

2. Under a hot broiler or over a gas stove burner, char the red and yellow bell peppers until their skins are uniformly blackened and blistered. Put them in a heatproof dish and cover

with a kitchen towel. When the peppers are cool enough to handle, peel off their charred skins. With a sharp knife, cut each pepper in half through its top and bottom and remove the stem, seeds, and ribs; then cut each half into quarters.

3. Bring a small saucepan of water to a boil. Cut off the green parts of 4 scallions and put them in the boiling water. Boil for 1 minute to blanch them, then drain and rinse under cold running water.

4. Place 1 blanched scallion on the inside of a chicken breast, then add a piece of yellow pepper and a piece of red pepper. Roll up the breast to enclose the peppers and scallion and tie it securely with kitchen string at both ends and in the middle. Repeat with the remaining breasts.

5. Preheat the oven to 400°F.

6. Heat a large, heavy ovenproof skillet over medium-high heat. Add the chicken breasts and brown them on all sides, 5 to 7 minutes. Put the skillet in the oven and roast the breasts until cooked through, about 15 minutes more. Remove and cover the skillet with foil to keep warm.

7. Halve the remaining scallions lengthwise and cut them into 1-inch pieces.

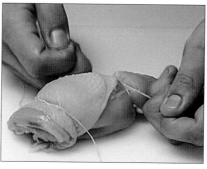

8. Heat the olive oil in a sauté pan over medium-high heat. Add the scallion pieces and sauté them for 1 minute. Add the vinegar and plum wine and boil until they are reduced by two thirds, 2 to 3 minutes. Stir in the cream and continue boiling until the mixture forms a sauce just thick enough to coat the back of a spoon, 2 to 3 minutes more. Reduce the heat to very low and, a little at a time, whisk in the butter. Season the sauce to taste with salt and pepper.

9. With a sharp knife, cut off the string from each rolled chicken breast. Cut each breast crosswise and at a slight angle into 6 slices and arrange them attractively in an overlapping fan on warmed serving plates or one large platter. Spoon the sauce over and around the chicken. Garnish with finely chopped chives.

Grilled Chicken Breasts with Garlic and Parsley

*G*rilled boneless chicken halves, simply seasoned with garlic and parsley and topped with garlic-lemon butter, have long been a **Spago** classic. The recipe becomes even simpler and quicker when you use boneless chicken breasts. Make sure you get the charcoal very hot and coated with gray ash before grilling the chicken. If you use a gas or electric grill, get it very hot, too, then turn down the heat

to medium just before you put the chicken breasts on. If you prefer, you could sauté or pan-roast the chicken breasts instead of grilling. Either way, serve them with your favorite vegetables, cooked al dente.

12 garlic cloves, peeled

1/4 cup flat-leaf parsley leaves

Salt

Freshly ground white pepper

4 boneless chicken breast halves,
  skin on

2 tablespoons unsalted butter

Juice of 1 large lemon

1 tablespoon finely chopped parsley

1. Bring a small saucepan of water to a boil. Add the garlic cloves and blanch them for 1 minute, then drain the garlic and, as soon as it is cool enough to handle, slice it thinly. Put the slices in a small bowl, add the parsley leaves and a little salt and white pepper, and toss them together.

2. With a finger, loosen a pocket between the skin and meat of each chicken breast, taking care not to separate the skin completely from the meat. Stuff about 2 teaspoons of the garlic-parsley mixture under the skin of each chicken breast. Place the chicken breasts on a

plate, cover with plastic wrap, and chill in the refrigerator until ready to use. Cover the remaining garlic-parsley mixture with plastic wrap and refrigerate it, too.

3. Heat a charcoal or gas grill until moderately hot. Grill the chicken breasts 6 to 8 minutes per side, just until cooked through, taking care not to overcook them.

4. While the chicken is grilling, melt the butter in a sauté pan and gently sauté the remaining garlic-parsley mixture just until it is fragrant. Stir in the lemon juice and chopped parsley and season to taste with salt and pepper.

5. As soon as the chicken breasts are done, place them on 4 large heated dinner plates. Spoon the sautéed garlic and parsley over each breast.

Grilled Italian Chicken with Summer Squash

..*H*ere's one of the simplest recipes I know for making great grilled chicken. Using a quickly prepared vinaigrette dressing as a marinade gives the poultry and vegetables an incredible burst of Mediterranean flavor and helps keep the meat extra juicy. For safety's sake, be sure to throw away the marinade after you've removed the food from it, and do not baste with it.

4 large boneless, skinless chicken
   breast halves
1 cup **Basil-Garlic Vinaigrette**
   (page 227)
2 medium zucchini, cut lengthwise
   into $1/4$-inch-thick slices

2 medium yellow summer squash,
   cut lengthwise into $1/4$-inch-thick
   slices
Salt
Freshly ground black pepper

1. Put the chicken breasts in a resealable plastic food storage bag. Pour ½ cup of the vinaigrette into the bag and seal it, pressing out as much air as possible. Place the zucchini and yellow squash slices in a separate bag, add the remaining vinaigrette, and seal. Refrigerate the bags of chicken and vegetables to marinate for at least 1 hour or as long as overnight.

2. Build a fire in a charcoal grill or preheat a gas grill,

a grill pan, or the broiler. Remove the chicken breasts and vegetables from the marinade and discard the marinade. Season the chicken and vegetables with salt and pepper.

3.   Grill or broil the chicken until cooked through and no longer pink when you cut into the thickest part of one breast, 8 to 10 minutes per side. After you've turned the chicken breasts over to cook on their second side, add the vegetable slices, carefully placing them lengthwise at right angles to the bars of the cooking grid. Grill the vegetables until golden brown and tender, 3 to 4 minutes per side. Fan grilled vegetable slices around the chicken. Garnish with fresh herbs.

Grilled Chicken Kebabs with Lemon and Thyme

*T*here's nothing like the smell of herb-scented smoke coming from an outdoor grill. One of the things I love about these kebabs is the way that a lemon wedge is grilled on each skewer. Carefully slid off the skewer and squeezed over the chunks of chicken, it delivers a wonderful, fragrant aroma. If you use wooden or bamboo skewers for the kebabs, be sure to soak them in water for about half an hour before you put food on them, to help keep them from scorching over the fire.

MARINADE

2 tablespoons extra-virgin olive oil

2 tablespoons lemon juice

1 small shallot, minced

2 teaspoons fresh thyme leaves

1 clove garlic, peeled and minced

1 teaspoon finely grated lemon zest

1/2 teaspoon salt

1/4 teaspoon freshly ground black pepper

4 large boneless, skinless, chicken breast halves

2 lemons, each cut into 4 wedges

1. In a medium bowl, whisk together the olive oil, lemon juice, shallot, thyme, garlic, lemon zest, salt, and pepper. Place in a large, resealable plastic food storage bag. Cut each chicken breast into about 8 large, equal-size chunks and add them to the bag with the marinade. Seal the bag, pressing out as much air as possible, and toss the ingredients in the bag to coat the chicken well. Refrigerate for about 1 hour.

2. Build a fire in a charcoal grill or preheat a gas grill, a grill pan, or the broiler. Remove the chicken chunks from the marinade and thread them onto 8 skewers, leaving a slight gap between each piece and including a lemon wedge on each skewer. Discard the marinade.

3. Grill the kebabs until the chicken is cooked through, 8 to 10 minutes total, turning the skewers once midway through. Serve 2 skewers per person.

Barbecued Butterflied Chicken
with Orange-Sherry Marinade

SERVES 4 TO 6

*B*utterflying a whole chicken—that is, splitting it along the backbone and then opening it out flat—makes the bird easy to grill quickly and evenly in one piece. You can do it yourself, following the simple directions in step 2 below, or ask the butcher to do it for you. In this recipe, I also share an easy-to-use secret for giving the chicken extra-crisp skin and moist, flavorful meat by stuffing some aromatics underneath the skin and then marinating the bird. Before cooking, be sure you place a drip pan under the grill beneath the chicken to reduce flare-ups.

2 large shallots, minced

2 large garlic cloves, peeled and
   minced

2 tablespoons minced fresh rosemary

1 chicken, 3¹/₂ to 4 pounds

MARINADE

¹/₂ cup freshly squeezed orange juice

¹/₄ cup orange marmalade

3 tablespoons sherry wine vinegar

2 tablespoons extra-virgin olive oil

Salt

Freshly ground black pepper

1. In a small bowl, stir together the shallots, garlic, and rosemary. Set aside.

2. To butterfly the chicken, first place it on a cutting board, breast up. Locate the backbone, which should be closest to the cutting surface. Insert a sharp, sturdy chef's knife into the bird's neck opening and carefully, firmly cut down along one side of the backbone through the thin rib bones,

all the way to the tail opening, then cut along the other side of the backbone to free it completely. Discard the backbone or freeze it and save it for stock. With your hands, open out the whole chicken, skin up, with the two cut edges from the backbone on either side. With the heels of your hands, press down firmly on the breast and ribs of the chicken to break the small bones and flatten the bird.

3. Using your fingertips, and inserting them through the neck-end opening, gently loosen the skin that covers the breast and thighs. Insert and spread about 1 tablespoon of the shallot mixture on each side of the chicken breast and on each thigh between the meat and the skin.

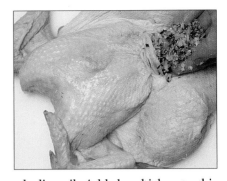

4. In a large, resealable plastic food storage bag or in a glass baking dish, stir together the remaining shallot mixture, orange juice, marmalade, vinegar, and olive oil. Add the chicken to this marinade, turning to coat it well. Reseal the bag, or cover the dish with plastic wrap. Marinate in the refrigerator at least 8 hours or overnight, turning the chicken occasionally.

5. Prepare a fire in a grill for the indirect cooking method: Push the hot coals to one side of a square or rectangular firebed, or around the perimeter of a circular one; or, with a gas grill, heat only one side of the firebed. Place a drip pan in the cooler area of the firebed, under the area where you'll place the chicken on the grill. Remove the chicken from the marinade, reserving the marinade. Season the chicken all over with salt and pepper.

6. Place the chicken skin side up on the grill rack directly over the drip pan. Brush the chicken with some of the reserved marinade. Close the grill lid, or place a large domed heatproof lid or baking pan over the chicken, and grill for about 40 minutes, checking the chicken every 10 minutes or so to make sure it's not burning. Turn the chicken skin side down and brush with more marinade; discard the remaining marinade. Cover again and grill the chicken until the juices run clear when the thickest part of a thigh is pierced, or the meat registers 170°F on an instant-read thermometer, 20 to 30 minutes longer.

7. With a sharp, heavy knife or cleaver, cut the chicken into 6 or 8 pieces. Arrange them on a bed of greens and serve immediately.

My Mother's Chicken-Stuffed Bell Peppers with Tomato Sauce

SERVES 6

I have to admit that when I was a kid growing up in the village of St. Viet in Austria, I didn't really like my mother's stuffed peppers. But as a grown-up, I love them, and I make them sometimes when I feel the need for old-fashioned comfort food. The chicken filling, which my mother always used, is a healthier alternative to the ground beef most people think of when stuffed peppers are mentioned. If you like, start with good-quality freshly ground chicken meat from the market rather than grinding it yourself. You'll need about a pound.

2 chicken legs, skin and bones removed, meat cut into even chunks	1 teaspoon chopped fresh thyme
	1 teaspoon salt, plus extra as needed
	1/2 teaspoon ground cumin
1/2 cup extra-virgin olive oil	Freshly ground white pepper, to taste
1 cup diced onion	2 cups cooked long-grain rice
1/2 pound mushrooms, finely chopped	5 cups My Favorite Tomato Sauce
2 garlic cloves, peeled and minced	(page 63), heated
1 egg, lightly beaten	6 green bell peppers
2 tablespoons chopped fresh parsley	Minced parsley, for garnish

1. With a meat grinder, or in a food processor fitted with the metal blade, coarsely grind the chicken. Transfer it to a mixing bowl and set aside.

2. In a medium skillet, heat ¼ cup of the olive oil over moderate heat. Add the onion and sauté until translucent, about 5 minutes. Add the mushrooms and continue to cook, stirring occasionally, until all the liquid given up by the mushrooms evaporates, 10 to 15 minutes. Set aside the mixture and let it cool.

3. Add the onion and mushrooms to the ground chicken. Add the garlic, egg, parsley, thyme, 1 teaspoon salt, cumin, and white pepper and mix well. To test for taste, sauté a small amount in a little oil and, when it is done, taste it and adjust the seasoning if necessary. Set the mixture aside and, when it is cool, stir in the cooked rice. Reserve.

4. While the chicken mixture cools, prepare My Favorite Tomato Sauce. Set it aside and keep warm.

5. Preheat the oven to 350°F.

6. Rinse the peppers under cold running water. Wipe them dry. Cut the top 1 inch from each pepper, keeping the stem intact, and reserve the tops. With your fingers and, if necessary, the tip of a small, sharp knife or a teaspoon, remove the core and seeds from each pepper. Brush the peppers inside and out with the remaining ¼ cup of olive oil. Season their insides with salt and pepper.

7. Divide the filling evenly among the peppers, filling them to the top. Place the lids back on top. In a baking dish just large enough to hold the peppers comfortably, arrange the stuffed peppers stem end up. Spoon the hot tomato sauce all around them. Bake in the preheated oven until the filling is cooked through and the peppers are tender, about 1 hour. With a serving spoon, transfer each pepper to a heated plate. Garnish with minced parsley.

All-American Chicken Pot Pie

■ ■ *C*ooking and eating chicken pot pie makes me feel all-American. It's so homey that it warms up any chilly evening. Of course, I couldn't leave the classic recipe alone. I've added Cheddar cheese and fresh chives to the crust to make it extra-delicious, and I've replaced the usual button mushrooms with meatier-tasting cremini or fresh shiitake mushrooms, which you can find in well-stocked produce sections and farmers' markets.

PASTRY

2 cups all-purpose flour

2 tablespoons snipped chives

12 tablespoons (1^1/2 sticks) unsalted
    butter, chilled, cut into small
    pieces

1 cup shredded sharp Cheddar cheese

2 egg yolks

5 to 6 tablespoons heavy cream

FILLING

2 tablespoons unsalted butter

1 tablespoon vegetable oil

1 pound boneless, skinless chicken
    breasts, cut into 1-inch pieces

2 medium carrots, cut into ^{1}/2-inch
    slices

1 stalk celery, cut into ^{1}/2-inch
    slices

^{1}/2 pound cremini or fresh shiitake
    mushrooms, stemmed and cut into
    ^{1}/2-inch slices

1 package frozen pearl onions,
    10 ounces, thawed

^{3}/4 cup frozen petits pois, thawed

SAUCE

6 tablespoons (^{3}/4 stick) unsalted
    butter

^{1}/4 cup all-purpose flour

1¹/₂ cups Chicken Stock (page 204) or good-quality canned chicken broth

¹/₂ cup heavy cream

1 teaspoon minced fresh thyme

Salt

Freshly ground black pepper

1 egg, beaten with 1 tablespoon water

1. To prepare the pastry: Put the flour and chives in a bowl. Using a pastry blender or your fingertips, work in the butter until the mixture resembles coarse crumbs. Add the cheese and toss it together with the flour mixture just until evenly mixed. In a small bowl, whisk together the egg yolks and 5 tablespoons of the cream. While stirring the flour-butter-cheese mixture continuously with a fork, sprinkle in the yolk-cream mixture a little at a time. If the mixture still seems a little too dry to hold together, add the remaining tablespoon of cream. With your hands, knead the dough lightly until it is just smooth. Press the dough into a thick, flat disk, wrap it in plastic wrap, and refrigerate until needed.

2. To prepare the filling: Heat a large skillet over medium-high heat and add the butter and vegetable oil. Add the chicken pieces and sauté just until lightly browned but not yet cooked through, 2 to 3 minutes. With a slotted spoon, remove the chicken to a mixing bowl. Leave the butter and oil in the skillet.

3. In the same skillet over medium-high heat, sauté the carrots, celery, and mushrooms, stirring frequently, until they begin to color, about 5 minutes. With a slotted spoon, remove them to a separate bowl. Stir the thawed pearl onions and petits pois into the other vegetables.

4. To prepare the sauce: In the same pan, melt the butter over medium heat. Add the flour and whisk until the mixture is smooth and bubbling, about 2 minutes. Remove the skillet from the heat and gradually whisk in the stock, cream, and thyme. Return the skillet to the heat and, stirring constantly, bring the mixture to a simmer. Cook, stirring continuously, until the sauce has thickened and is smooth, about 2 minutes. Season to taste with salt and

pepper. Stir in the reserved chicken and vegetables. Set the pan aside and let the mixture cool for about 20 minutes.

5. Meanwhile, preheat the oven to 400°F.

6. Spoon the cooled filling into a 10-inch deep-dish pie plate. On a lightly floured surface, roll out the dough into an even circle 11 inches in diameter. Loosely roll up the dough around the rolling pin, then transfer it to the pie plate and unroll it on top. With a small, sharp knife, trim the uneven edge of the dough slightly, reserving the trimmings; then, fold the overhang underneath and press it gently all around the rim of the baking dish to make a decorative rim. If you like, gather up the trimmings into a ball, roll them out again, and cut them into decorative designs to apply to the top of the pie. Brush pastry with the beaten egg wash. Using the tip of the knife, cut three slits in the center of the pie dough.

7. Bake the pie until the crust is golden brown and the filling beneath is bubbling hot, 25 to 30 minutes. Present the pie at the table on a trivet and use a big metal pie server and a big spoon to cut and scoop the crust and filling onto each heated plate.

Wiener Backhendl

SERVES 4

*D*on't worry about the fancy-sounding Austrian name. It's just good old-fashioned fried chicken, made the way I loved to eat it when I was a boy. My sons, **Byron** and **Cameron**, love it, too. Because most people today don't like skin underneath the coating on their fried chicken, I remove it, but I leave in the bones for extra flavor and moistness. For really crunchy results, I like to use the Japanese-style bread crumbs known as panko, which are very jagged; but regular bread crumbs will work just fine, too. Serve the chicken with a mixed green salad, in the Austrian style, or with mashed potatoes (pages 160–62).

2¹/₂ pounds chicken, cut into pieces for frying

Salt

Freshly ground black pepper

2 cups all-purpose flour

3 eggs, beaten

4 cups panko or bread crumbs

Vegetable oil for deep-frying

1 cup whole parsley leaves, rinsed and thoroughly dried

2 lemons, cut into halves

1. Remove the skin from the chicken pieces but leave the bones in. Season the chicken generously with salt and pepper. On 3 separate soup plates, put the flour, the eggs, and the panko or bread crumbs.

2. In a deep-fryer or a large, deep, heavy skillet, heat several inches of vegetable oil to 350°F on a deep-frying thermometer.

3. One piece at a time, dip the chicken into and coat it evenly with the flour, then the egg, and then the bread crumbs. Gently shake off excess crumbs and set the chicken pieces aside.

4. As soon as the oil is hot, carefully put the chicken in the oil and deep-fry until golden brown and cooked through, 12 to 14 minutes, using a wire skimmer or slotted spoon to turn the pieces so they cook evenly. With the skimmer or spoon, remove them from the oil when done and transfer to paper towels to drain.

5. Immediately put the parsley into the hot oil and fry until dark green and crisp, about 30 seconds. Remove it with the skimmer or slotted spoon and drain on paper towels.

6. Divide the chicken pieces among serving plates and scatter the fried parsley on top. Serve immediately with lemon halves for squeezing over the chicken.

Turkey Mushroom Burgers with Chunky Tomato Salsa Compote

SERVES 8

*P*eople love turkey or chicken burgers today because they're so lean. But that lack of fat can also make them dry. I solve that problem by adding a moist puree of cooked mushrooms, which also gives the burgers even more flavor. Because you wouldn't want to eat a poultry burger anything other than well done, it's a good idea to shape them thinner than a beef burger so they'll cook fairly quickly without losing too much moisture. Try the special technique I give below for shaping thin burger patties without risk of them falling apart.

TURKEY MUSHROOM BURGERS

2 tablespoons extra-virgin olive oil

1/4 pound (1 stick) unsalted butter

3 garlic cloves, peeled and minced

1 teaspoon minced onion

1 bay leaf

1 pound button mushrooms, finely chopped

1 pound portobello mushrooms, stemmed and cut into 1/4-inch dice

Salt

Freshly ground black pepper

1/4 cup chopped fresh thyme

1/4 cup chopped fresh oregano

2 pounds ground turkey

CHUNKY TOMATO SALSA COMPOTE

1 cup Tomato Concassé (page 217)

1/4 cup minced red onion

1/4 cup minced green onion

1/4 cup minced fresh cilantro

3 tablespoons lime juice

2 tablespoons minced jalapeño chili

2 tablespoons vegetable oil

1 tablespoon honey

1/2 teaspoon salt

2 tablespoons extra-virgin olive oil, for oiling the grill rack or heating in a skillet

8 hamburger buns

10 ounces queso fresco (Mexican fresh white cheese) or other mild white cheese, crumbled or shredded

Thinly sliced red onion

Romaine lettuce leaves

1. Heat a large sauté pan over medium-high heat. Add the olive oil and butter and, when the butter has melted, add the garlic, onion, and bay leaf and sauté until fragrant, 1 minute. Add the mushrooms, season with salt and pepper to taste, and cook, stirring frequently, until most of the liquid released by the mushrooms has evaporated and the mixture looks almost dry, 10 to 15 minutes. Stir in the thyme and oregano. Remove from the heat and let the mixture cool to room temperature. Remove the bay leaf.

2. Put the turkey in a large mixing bowl and add the cooled mushroom mixture. Stir with a wooden spoon, or mix with your hands, until the turkey and mushrooms are thoroughly combined. Mix in salt and pepper to taste.

3. Divide the mixture into 8 equal portions, forming each into a compact, even ball. To form each patty, place a sheet of plastic wrap about 12 inches long on a work surface and brush it with some olive oil. Put a ball of turkey mixture in the center of one half of the sheet and fold the other half over it. With the back of a plate, press down on the ball to flatten it to an even patty about ¾ inch thick. Repeat with the remaining balls. Refrigerate until ready to cook.

4. To make the Chunky Tomato Salsa Compote: In a small saucepan, combine the Tomato Concassé, red and green onion, cilantro, lime juice, jalapeño, vegetable oil, honey, and salt. Bring to a boil over medium-high heat. Reduce the heat to a simmer and cook, stirring occasionally, until most of the liquid has evaporated, about 10 minutes.

5. Build a fire in a charcoal grill or preheat a gas grill, grill pan, or the broiler. Just before cooking, use the oil to grease the grill's cooking grid, or heat a large skillet over medium-high heat and add the olive oil. Remove the plastic wrap from the turkey burgers and grill, broil, or pan-fry them until cooked through, 4 to 5 minutes per side.

6. With a spatula, transfer the turkey burgers to the bottom halves of the buns. Top each burger with a generous spoonful of the Chunky Tomato Salsa Compote, some fresh white cheese, sliced red onion, and a romaine leaf. Serve immediately.

Wolfgang's Bacon-Wrapped Meat Loaf

Spicy Asian Beef Burgers with Shiitake Mushrooms

New York Steaks with Four Peppercorns and Port Wine Sauce

Beef Stew with Winter Vegetables and Red Wine

My Beef Goulash

Roasted Beef Tenderloin with Smoky Tomato-Chili Salsa

Wiener Schnitzel with Warm Potato Salad

Minced Veal or Pork with Chanterelles, Paprika Cream Sauce,
    and Noodles

Rack of Pork with Caramelized Maple Onions

Fresh Sweet Italian Fennel Sausage

Catalonian Fire-Roasted Rack of Lamb

Chinois Grilled Lamb Chops with Cilantro-Mint Vinaigrette

Wolfgang's Bacon-Wrapped Meat Loaf

*G*uests in my **Wolfgang Puck Cafes** love this dish, probably because it reminds them of home cooking and their grandmothers! The bacon helps keep the meat loaf moist and flavorful. Moisture is a key concern and one of the reasons that I also recommend baking the meat loaf gently and slowly in a water bath, made by setting the loaf pan inside a baking pan filled with water in the oven. Serve with mashed potatoes (pages 160–62), or either hot or cold in a sandwich made with my Focaccia (page 172).

3 tablespoons extra-virgin olive oil	1½ teaspoons salt
1 large onion, peeled and diced	½ teaspoon freshly ground black
½ pound mushrooms, trimmed and	pepper
finely chopped	1 pound lean ground beef
3 large cloves garlic, peeled and	1 pound lean ground pork
minced	1 pound ground veal
1 cup heavy cream	1 egg, lightly beaten
1½ teaspoons minced fresh oregano	¾ pound sliced smoked bacon
1½ teaspoons minced fresh thyme	(about 13 slices)

1. In a large skillet over medium-high heat, heat the olive oil. Sauté the onion until translucent, about 8 minutes. Add the mushrooms and garlic and cook over medium-high heat until they just begin to color, 3 to 5 minutes. Stir in the cream, oregano, thyme, salt, and pepper. Bring the mixture to a boil, then reduce the heat and simmer until the vegetables

are tender, about 5 minutes. Transfer the vegetable mixture to a large mixing bowl and let it cool.

2. Preheat the oven to 400°F. Add to the bowl the beef, pork, and veal. Stir in the egg and continue mixing just until the ingredients are thoroughly combined.

3. On a work surface, position a 9 by 5 by 3-inch loaf pan. Line the bottom and sides of the pan with the bacon slices, placing them parallel to the short end and slightly overlapping, with their ends hanging over the edges. Add the meat mixture to the pan, patting it down to make it smooth and even. Fold the ends of the bacon strips up and over the meat mixture to enclose it completely. Cover the loaf pan with aluminum foil.

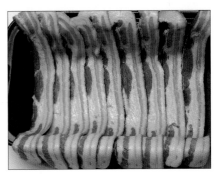

4. To prepare the water bath, place a roasting pan inside the oven on the middle shelf. Bring a kettle of water to a boil. Using an oven glove, slide out partway from the oven the shelf with the roasting pan. Place the loaf pan in the center of the roasting pan. Carefully pour boiling water into the roasting pan to come halfway up the side of the loaf pan. Cover the roasting pan with aluminum foil.

5. Carefully slide the shelf back into the oven and bake for 1 hour. Remove the foil and continue to bake until an instant-read thermometer inserted into the center of the meat loaf registers 165°F, about 30 minutes more.

6. Remove the pan of meat loaf from the oven and let it rest for 10 minutes. Meanwhile, carefully empty the boiling water from the roasting pan. Holding the loaf pan with oven gloves or pot holders, carefully pour the juices from the pan into a sauceboat or heatproof cup. Cut the loaf crosswise into 8 slices, taking care to cut completely through the bacon with each slice. Serve each slice drizzled with pan juices.

Spicy Asian Beef Burgers with Shiitake Mushrooms

SERVES 4

*T*he next time you want to liven things up at a casual barbecue, try these unusual burgers. They aren't too spicy, but they are delicious and different. Most markets with good produce sections now carry fresh shiitake mushrooms. If you like teriyaki sauce, warm a little extra to spoon over each burger at serving time. And here's a tip for people who like their beef burgers on the rarer side: shape them a little bit thicker, so they'll still be good and pink in the center when their outsides are nicely grilled.

2 pounds ground beef

1/4 cup minced garlic

2 1/2 tablespoons chopped fresh
   cilantro leaves

4 teaspoons thinly sliced scallions

1 teaspoon curry powder

1 teaspoon ground cumin

1 teaspoon sugar

2 small hot fresh chili peppers,
   stemmed, seeded, and minced

Salt

Freshly ground black pepper

2 bunches scallions, cut into 3-inch-
   long pieces

8 fresh shiitake mushrooms, stemmed

Olive oil or vegetable oil, for grilling

1/4 cup bottled teriyaki sauce, plus
   extra if desired

4 sesame-seed hamburger buns

1. In a mixing bowl, combine the beef, garlic, cilantro, sliced scallions, curry powder, cumin, sugar, chilies, and salt and pepper to taste. Mix well. With your hands, form the mixture into 4 equal patties slightly wider in diameter than the burger buns. Set aside on a clean plate, cover with plastic wrap, and refrigerate until ready to cook.

2. Build a fire in a charcoal grill or preheat an outdoor or indoor gas or electric grill or the broiler.

3. Just before cooking, put the scallion pieces and shiitake mushrooms in a bowl and drizzle them with enough oil to coat them lightly. Brush the grill's cooking surface with a little more oil to prevent sticking. Place the burger patties on the grill and cook until done to your liking, 4 to 5 minutes per side for medium. When you turn the burgers over, add the scallions and shiitakes to the grill and immediately brush the burgers and the vegetables

with the teriyaki sauce. A minute or so before the food is done, brush the cut sides of the buns with a little oil and place them cut side down on the grill to warm and toast lightly.

4. When the burgers are done and the scallions and shiitakes are nicely browned, remove them and the buns from the grill. Place a burger on the bottom half of each bun and top with scallions and shiitake mushrooms. Serve immediately.

New York Steaks with Four Peppercorns and Port Wine Sauce

*T*he distinctive flavors of four different types of peppercorns give this classic French-style steak its special flavor. But the real secret to any successful steak recipe is to look for the best-quality meat you can find. I love Creamy Mashed Potatoes with Caramelized Onions (page 160) on the side.

1 cup port or dry sherry

2 tablespoons whole pink peppercorns

2 tablespoons whole green peppercorns

2 tablespoons whole black peppercorns

2 tablespoons whole white peppercorns

6 New York steaks, about 8 ounces each

Salt

2 tablespoons mild-flavored oil, such as almond or safflower oil

1 cup heavy cream

1/2 cup Brown Veal Stock (page 207) or good-quality canned beef broth

3 tablespoons unsalted butter, cut into small pieces

1. The night before you make the dish, put the port or sherry in a nonreactive bowl. Add the pink and green peppercorns, cover, and leave to soak overnight.

2. Before cooking, fold the black and white peppercorns inside a clean napkin or put them in

a heavy-duty plastic bag. With a rolling pin, roll over the napkin or bag to crush the peppercorns coarsely.

3. With a sharp knife, trim any excess fat from the steaks. Season them to taste with salt and sprinkle both sides with the crushed peppercorns, using your palm to press them into the meat.

4. Heat a large, heavy skillet over high heat. Pour in the oil and cook the steaks until done to your liking, about 4 minutes each side for medium-rare. Set the steaks aside and keep them warm.

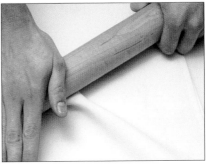

5. Pour out the fat from the pan. Add the port or sherry with the pink and green peppercorns and, over high heat, stir and scrape to deglaze the pan deposits. Simmer the port or sherry until it has reduced by about half, 7 to 10 minutes. Stir in the cream and stock and continue simmering briskly until the sauce is thick enough to coat the back of a spoon. Reduce the heat and whisk in the butter, one small piece at a time. Season to taste with salt.

6. Place one steak on each warmed serving plate. Ladle the sauce over the steaks, dividing the peppercorns equally over each portion.

Beef Stew with Winter Vegetables and Red Wine

SERVES 4

*T*here's nothing more comforting and delicious on a cold winter day than a big, lovingly simmered beef stew. Pick a flavorful, tougher cut of beef like chuck, which turns tender during the stew's slow, gentle cooking.

2 pounds beef chuck

1/4 cup all-purpose flour

1 teaspoon kosher salt, plus
   additional as needed

1/4 teaspoon freshly ground black
   pepper, plus additional as needed

3 tablespoons vegetable oil

2 tablespoons unsalted butter

1 large onion, cut into 1/2-inch chunks

2 large garlic cloves, peeled and
   minced

1/2 cup dry red wine

2 cups good-quality beef broth,
   homemade or canned

1/4 cup balsamic vinegar

1 bay leaf

6 to 8 large fresh sage leaves, washed
   and dried

1 pound butternut squash, peeled and
   cut into 1-inch chunks

1/2 pound parsnips, peeled and cut
   into 1-inch chunks

2 medium carrots, peeled and cut into
   1-inch chunks

1/2 pound Roma tomatoes, peeled,
   cored, seeded, and diced (page 217)

Chopped parsley, for garnish

1. Cut the beef into 1-inch cubes, trimming away any gristle or excess fat.
2. On a piece of waxed paper or in a plastic food storage bag, combine the flour, salt, and pepper. Turn the beef cubes in the flour mixture to coat them evenly, or place them in the food storage bag and shake until they are coated.
3. In a wide, heavy saucepan, heat the oil over medium-high heat. Add the beef cubes and sauté until evenly browned on all sides, 5 to 7 minutes. Remove the beef and set it aside.
4. Reduce the heat to medium and, in the same saucepan, melt the butter. Add the onion and garlic and sauté until translucent, about 3 minutes.

5. Add the red wine and, with a wooden spoon, stir and scrape to deglaze the pan deposits. Return the meat to the pan. Add the stock, vinegar, and bay leaf. Reduce the heat to low, cover the pan, and simmer gently for 1 hour.

6. Cut the sage leaves into chiffonade strips (page 229) and stir them into the sauce along with the butternut squash, parsnips, carrots, and tomatoes. Cover the pan again and continue simmering until both the meat and the vegetables are tender, about 30 minutes longer. Remove the bay leaf and correct the seasonings with salt and pepper to taste. Ladle the stew into large warmed bowls and garnish with chopped parsley.

My Beef Goulash

SERVES 6

*G*oulash, of course, comes from Hungary and is probably its most famous dish. But that country is close enough to my native Austria that I grew up loving the stew. The most important ingredient is the paprika, which gives it a rich, mildly spicy, toasty flavor. Look for paprika imported from Hungary and buy a new container from the market, throwing out that musty tin that's been sitting for years in your pantry. I always serve goulash with Spaetzle (page 165), those wonderful little dumplings from Austria. The goulash is also excellent with egg noodles, rice, or boiled potatoes.

2 tablespoons extra-virgin olive oil

4 cups thinly sliced onions

1 tablespoon sugar

3 garlic cloves, peeled and minced

1 tablespoon caraway seeds, toasted
    and ground (page 222)

1¹/₂ tablespoons sweet or mild
    paprika

1 teaspoon hot paprika

2 tablespoons minced fresh marjoram
    leaves

1 teaspoon minced fresh thyme leaves

1 bay leaf

3 tablespoons tomato paste

4 cups Chicken Stock (page 204) or
    good-quality canned chicken broth

2 tablespoons balsamic vinegar

2¹/₂ pounds boneless beef shank,
    trimmed and cut into 2-inch cubes

1 teaspoon kosher salt, plus
    additional as needed

¹/₄ teaspoon freshly ground black
    pepper, plus additional as needed

1. In a large sauté pan, heat the olive oil over medium heat. Add the onions and sprinkle in the sugar. Sauté, stirring frequently, until the onions are caramelized a golden brown, about 15 minutes. Add the garlic and caraway seeds and sauté until fragrant, about 1 minute more. Add both paprikas, the marjoram, thyme, and bay leaf and sauté until fragrant, another minute or so.

2. Add the tomato paste. Pour in the Chicken Stock and vinegar and stir and scrape with a wooden spoon to deglaze the pan deposits. Add the pieces of beef, 1 teaspoon of the salt,

and ¼ teaspoon of the pepper. Raise the heat slightly and bring the liquid to a boil. Then, lower the heat to maintain a bare simmer and cook, covered, until the beef is very tender, 1½ to 2 hours, stirring occasionally.

3. Taste and adjust the seasoning with salt and pepper. Serve immediately.

Roasted Beef Tenderloin with
Smoky Tomato-Chili Salsa

SERVES 4

*T*he salsa's combination of cool tomato and spicy chili pepper flavors is fabulous with the roast beef. Because this recipe calls for a relatively small cut that roasts quickly, I give the beef extra flavor by pan-searing it before I put it in the oven. The coriander seeds I use to season the beef add a wonderful aroma, especially when you start with whole seeds and toast and crush

them. In a pinch, you can substitute already ground coriander, but don't use it from a jar that's been sitting forever in your pantry. **Potato Galette with Goat Cheese (page 163) makes an excellent side dish.**

TOMATO-CHILI SALSA

5 Roma tomatoes, cored

2 canned chipotle (smoked jalapeño) chilies

1/2 cup fresh lime juice

1/2 cup chopped fresh basil

1/4 cup minced garlic

1/4 cup balsamic vinegar

2 teaspoons sugar

2 teaspoons salt, plus additional as needed

1/2 teaspoon freshly ground black pepper, plus additional as needed

1 cup plus 2 tablespoons extra-virgin olive oil

1 tablespoon whole coriander seeds

2 1/2 pounds beef tenderloin, trimmed

1. To prepare the Tomato-Chili Salsa: Over a hot grill, on a grill pan, or under the broiler, roast the tomatoes until blackened, turning them frequently as their skin blisters, about 15

minutes. Transfer to a nonreactive mixing bowl and add the chipotle chilies. Cover and allow to cool for 15 minutes. Add the lime juice, basil, and garlic and marinate for 10 minutes. Transfer the mixture to a blender or food processor and pulse until chunky. Transfer to a bowl and stir in the vinegar, sugar, 2 teaspoons of the salt, and ½ teaspoon of the pepper. Whisking continuously,  slowly pour in 1 cup of the olive oil. Cover with plastic wrap and refrigerate until serving time.

2. Put the coriander seeds in a small, dry saucepan. Over medium heat, toast the seeds, stirring them continuously, just until they are fragrant, 1 to 2 minutes. Immediately transfer the seeds to a small bowl to cool. Then crush them with a mortar and pestle or in a spice mill. Season the beef all over with the coriander and with salt and pepper to taste. Set aside.

3. Preheat the oven to 400°F.

4. In an ovenproof sauté pan over high heat, heat the remaining two tablespoons of olive oil until it is almost smoking. Add the beef and sear it until browned all over, about 5 minutes. Transfer the pan to the oven and roast until medium rare, 130°F on a meat thermometer inserted into its thickest part, 12 to 15 minutes. Remove the pan from the oven, cover with foil, and let the meat rest for 10 minutes. Then, with a sharp knife, cut it across the grain into ¼-inch-thick slices and place the slices overlapping on heated serving plates. Serve immediately, spooning the salsa alongside the meat or passing it separately.

Wiener Schnitzel with Warm Potato Salad

SERVES 4

*I*n Vienna, an old piece of folk wisdom says that a perfectly fried veal schnitzel should be so free of grease that a gentleman could sit down on it and the schnitzel wouldn't even leave a stain on his trousers. I think there are better things to do with Wiener schnitzel, especially enjoying it with a **Warm Potato Salad** as guests do at Spago and in my Wolfgang Puck Cafes. Buy the veal scaloppine from a reliable butcher and ask for them good and thin, no more than 1/4-inch thick; if necessary, at home, put each one between 2 sheets of plastic wrap and pound with a meat mallet to make them even thinner. To give the schnitzels an extra-crisp coating, look for the packaged, coarse Japanese-style bread crumbs known as panko. You'll find the small, slender potatoes descriptively called fingerlings in well-stocked produce departments and farmers' markets; or substitute any good, small, waxy potatoes such as delicious, buttery-tasting Yukon golds, cooking them a little longer, depending on their size.

WARM POTATO SALAD

1 cup Champagne vinegar

1/4 cup peanut oil

3 tablespoons sugar

2 1/2 tablespoons kosher salt

1 tablespoon finely chopped fresh
   thyme leaves

1/2 teaspoon freshly ground black
   pepper

1 small yellow onion, cut into 1/4-inch
   dice

1 pound fingerling potatoes, washed

3 whole peeled garlic cloves

3 sprigs of fresh parsley

WIENER SCHNITZEL

Peanut oil for deep-frying

1 cup all-purpose flour

2 eggs, beaten with 2 tablespoons
   cold water

4 cups panko or fresh dry white bread
   crumbs

4 veal scaloppine, 8 ounces each

Salt

Freshly ground black pepper

1 cup whole parsley leaves, rinsed
   and thoroughly dried

2 lemons, each cut into 4 wedges

1. To prepare the Warm Potato Salad: In a nonreactive mixing bowl, combine the vinegar, peanut oil, sugar, ½ tablespoon of the kosher salt, and the thyme, pepper, and onion. Whisk until well blended. Set aside.

2. In a large saucepan, combine the potatoes, garlic, parsley, and remaining 2 tablespoons salt. Add enough cold water to cover the potatoes completely. Bring the water to a boil over high heat, then reduce the heat to maintain a simmer and cook until the potatoes are just tender enough to be pierced easily with a knife tip, 8 to 10 minutes. Do not overcook them. Drain the potatoes. When they are cool enough to handle, cut them crosswise into ¼-inch-thick round slices, add them to the bowl containing the dressing, and toss thoroughly but gently. Leave them to marinate for at least 20 minutes before serving.

3. To make the Wiener schnitzel: In a deep, heavy skillet or saucepan, preheat about 3 inches of oil to 375°F on a deep-frying thermometer.

4. Put the flour, egg mixture, and bread crumbs in each of three large, shallow pie plates or soup plates, side by side. Season the veal scaloppine on both sides with salt and pepper. One at a time, dredge the scaloppine in flour to coat them evenly; then dip them on both sides in egg wash; then turn them in the panko or bread crumbs to coat them evenly. Gently shake off excess crumbs. On a work surface, use a sharp knife to lightly score the breading four times in a crosshatch pattern, to help secure the breading and prevent curling. Carefully slip the scaloppine into the hot oil and deep-fry until golden on both sides, about 3 minutes. Remove with a wire skimmer or slotted spoon and transfer to paper towels to drain.

5. While the schnitzels are frying, put the potato salad in a sauté pan and, over high heat, quickly rewarm it. Spoon the potato salad onto each of 4 warmed serving plates.

6. As soon as the schnitzels are done frying, put the parsley into the hot oil and fry until dark green and crisp, 15 to 20 seconds. Remove it with the skimmer or slotted spoon and drain on paper towels.

7. Place a Wiener schnitzel on each plate, partly overlapping the potato salad. Garnish with fried parsley leaves and lemon wedges and serve immediately.

Minced Veal or Pork with Chanterelles, Paprika Cream Sauce, and Noodles

*I*t's so much easier to say "minced veal" than "Kalbs Geschnetzeltes," the Austrian name for this dish, which I demonstrated as part of my **Food Network** cooking show devoted to the Austrian Alpine town of Salzburg, birthplace of Mozart. **Eastern European comfort food at its best, the recipe combines bite-size pieces of tender veal, whole mushrooms, paprika, and a rich cream sauce. Like most home-style recipes, this simple one is infinitely adaptable. You could substitute pork, chicken, or turkey for the veal, and regular button mushrooms for the trumpet-shaped golden chanterelles that are now commercially cultivated and sold in upscale produce departments and farmers' markets.**

4 tablespoons vegetable oil

2 pounds veal tenderloin or pork tenderloin, cut into bite-size $^1/_4$-inch-thick slices

Salt

6 tablespoons ($^3/_4$ stick) unsalted butter

1 onion, finely chopped

3 cloves garlic, peeled and minced

1 pound chanterelles, trimmed

1 teaspoon sweet paprika

$^1/_4$ teaspoon hot paprika

1 cup heavy cream

1 pound wide egg noodles

2 tablespoons minced fresh parsley leaves, plus extra for garnish

1 tablespoon minced fresh marjoram leaves

Freshly ground black pepper

2 tablespoons crème fraîche or sour cream

1. Rest a strainer on top of a mixing bowl and set aside. Heat a heavy sauté pan over high heat. Add the oil and, as soon as you begin to see slight wisps of smoke, add the meat and sear it until it is evenly browned, breaking up the meat with a wooden spoon, 5 to 7 minutes. Empty the meat from the skillet into the strainer; the juices will drain into the bowl. Reserve the meat and juices separately.

2. Bring a large pot of salted water to a boil.

3. Still over high heat, add 3 tablespoons of the butter to the pan. When it begins to turn brown, add the onion, garlic, chanterelles, and paprikas. Sauté, stirring frequently, until all the liquid given up by the mushrooms has evaporated, 7 to 10 minutes. Add the heavy cream and reserved meat juices. Bring to a boil and continue boiling until the liquid has thickened slightly, about 5 minutes.

4. While the sauce is cooking, add the noodles to the pot of boiling water. Cook them until al dente, tender but still slightly chewy, following the manufacturer's suggested cooking time. Drain the noodles well. In another sauté pan or saucepan, melt the remaining butter over medium-low heat. Add the drained noodles and toss them well with the butter.

5. Add to the sauce the reserved meat, parsley, and marjoram and season to taste with salt and pepper. Simmer briefly until the meat is heated through. Stir in the crème fraîche.

6. Mound the buttered noodles on individual heated serving plates or shallow soup plates. Spoon the meat, mushrooms, and sauce over the noodles, garnish with parsley, and serve immediately.

Rack of Pork with Caramelized Maple Onions

▪▪ *P*ork is naturally such a sweet-tasting and robust meat that it goes very well with seasonings and sauces that are also sweet and have real depth of flavor. Maple syrup is a perfect example, especially when it's paired with caramelized onions. You'll be surprised by how complex and exciting this simple dish tastes. Serve over mashed potatoes (pages 160–62) or rice to sop up the juices.

1 rack of pork, 2 pounds, with bones attached

Salt

Freshly ground black pepper

1/4 cup extra-virgin olive oil

3 tablespoons unsalted butter

2 large yellow onions, peeled and sliced

2 tablespoons finely chopped fresh ginger

1/2 cinnamon stick

1 whole star anise

1/4 cup maple syrup

2 cups apple cider

1. About 20 minutes before cooking, season both sides of the pork rack with salt and pepper. Set aside at room temperature.

2. In a large, heavy skillet over high heat, heat the olive oil. Sear the pork rack on all sides until evenly browned, 5 to 7 minutes. Remove the pork and set aside.

3. Preheat the oven to 350°F.

4. Reduce the heat under the skillet to medium and add the butter. When it has melted, add the onions, ginger, cinnamon stick, and star anise. Sauté, stirring frequently, until the onions are golden brown, about 10 minutes. Stir in the maple syrup and continue sautéing, stirring continuously, until the mixture has a deep caramel color, about 2 minutes more.

5. Add the cider to the pan and stir and scrape with a wooden spoon to deglaze the pan deposits. Season to taste with salt and pepper and continue cooking until the liquid has reduced by half, about 5 minutes. Remove and discard the cinnamon stick and star anise.

6. Transfer the pork to a small roasting pan or baking dish and cover it with half of the onion mixture. Roast the pork until a roasting thermometer inserted into its thickest part not touching bone registers 160°F, about 40 minutes, covering it with the remaining onion mixture halfway through roasting.

7. When the pork is done, remove it from the oven, cover the dish with foil, and let the pork rest for 10 minutes so the meat juices settle. With a sharp knife, carve the pork between the bones into 4 chops. Serve on heated plates, spooning the onions and pan juices over and around the pork.

Fresh Sweet Italian Fennel Sausage

MAKES ABOUT 5 POUNDS SAUSAGE, 10 TO 12 SERVINGS

*I*f you really love fresh sausage, as I do, then nothing beats making it yourself. This particular version features popular Italian-style seasonings and yields a generous amount for a party. You could cut the quantities in half or quarter them for a smaller meal. Leave a little fat on the meat to keep the sausages moist and juicy. A meat grinder makes it easy to achieve the perfect sausage

texture, but, in a pinch, a food processor fitted with the metal blade will also work. Poaching the sausages in a quick, simple **Court Bouillon** before you brown them keeps them incredibly moist. Mashed potatoes (pages 160–62) or potato salad (page 48) are ideal accompaniments.

5 pounds pork butt, trimmed and cut into 1-inch cubes	1 tablespoon mild paprika
4 tablespoons salt	1 1/2 teaspoons cayenne pepper
2 teaspoons freshly ground black pepper	3/4 cup **Chicken Stock** (page 204) or good-quality canned chicken broth, iced
2 tablespoons whole fennel seeds, toasted (page 222)	2 quarts **Court Bouillon** (page 208)
1/4 cup chopped garlic	1/4 cup extra-virgin olive oil
1/4 cup plus 2 tablespoons sugar	Honey mustard
	Minced onion, for garnish

1. In a mixing bowl, combine the pork, salt, black pepper, fennel seeds, garlic, sugar, paprika, and cayenne pepper. Toss well to distribute all the seasonings evenly among the meat cubes. Cover the bowl with plastic wrap and put in the freezer for 30 minutes.

2. To grind the sausage, push the mixture through a meat grinder using the large-hole plate.

Alternatively, working in batches, pulse the meat mixture in a food processor fitted with the metal blade until coarsely but evenly chopped. Transfer the mixture to the bowl of an electric mixer and, using the paddle attachment on the lowest speed, mix for 1 minute; then increase the speed to medium, slowly pour in the stock, and mix for 2 minutes more; finally, switch to high speed and mix for 30 seconds. Alternatively, in batches, pulse the stock into the mixture in the food processor.

3. To form a sausage, place a 12 by 16-inch piece of plastic wrap on a work surface. About 6 inches from one narrow end, place 1 cup of the meat mixture, fold the 6 inches of plastic wrap over it, and pat the meat into an 8 by 1½-inch cylinder. Roll up the meat tightly in the plastic and knot the ends on either side of the meat to seal it in. Wrap the plastic-wrapped sausage securely in aluminum foil. Repeat with the remaining sausage meat.

4. In a large sauté pan or saucepan, bring the Court Bouillon to a simmer. Add the prepared sausages and poach them until firm, about 10 minutes. With a slotted spoon or wire skimmer, remove the sausages from the liquid and leave them at room temperature just until cool enough to handle. Carefully peel off their foil and plastic wrappers.

5. In a heavy sauté pan over high heat, heat the olive oil. Add the sausages and sauté them just until nicely browned on all sides, 4 to 5 minutes. Serve immediately with honey mustard and minced onion.

Catalonian Fire-Roasted Rack of Lamb

My friend Lydia Shire, the great Boston-based chef, introduced this special-occasion dish to me when she and several other top American chefs—including Nobu Matsuhisa, Charlie Palmer, Joachim Splichal, and François Payard—joined me in the kitchen at Spago for a charity dinner a few years ago. Two dynamic sources of flavor bring incredible excitement to the lamb: a marinade flavored with shallots, garlic, ancho chilies, cilantro, and lime juice; and a classic **Catalan Romesco sauce** fragrant with sweet and hot peppers, tomatoes, garlic, olive oil, saffron, and toasted almonds.

MARINADE

1/2 cup plus 3 tablespoons extra-virgin
    olive oil

3 shallots, sliced

8 garlic cloves, peeled and sliced

1 dry ancho chili, toasted and crushed
    (page 222)

2 scallions, thinly sliced

1 small handful of fresh cilantro
    leaves

Juice of 2 or 3 limes

1 tablespoon honey

3 racks of lamb, chine bone removed,
    rib bones removed and reserved

Salt

Freshly ground black pepper

ROMESCO SAUCE

3/4 cup extra-virgin olive oil

10 garlic cloves, peeled and
    chopped

4 whole tomatoes, cut in half

3 shallots, sliced

2 dry ancho chilies, toasted and
    crushed (page 222)

1 serrano or jalapeño chili, stemmed,
    seeded, and chopped

1 red bell pepper, stemmed, seeded,
    and diced

1 tablespoon cumin seeds, toasted and crushed (page 222)	1/4 cup fresh basil leaves
1 tablespoon coriander seeds, toasted and crushed (page 222)	1/4 cup fresh parsley leaves
Large pinch of saffron threads	1 cup tomato juice
3/4 cup sliced almonds, toasted (page 221)	Juice of 1 or 2 limes
	Salt
	Freshly ground black pepper

1. To prepare the marinade: Heat a heavy skillet over high heat and add the ½ cup of olive oil. Sauté the shallots, garlic, and ancho chili until the shallots and garlic just begin to turn golden, about 2 minutes. Remove from the heat and stir in the scallions, cilantro leaves, lime juice, and honey. Transfer the marinade to a nonreactive dish, add the boneless whole rack of lamb, cover, and leave in the refrigerator to marinate for 2 hours.

2. Preheat the oven to 400°F.

3. To prepare the Romesco Sauce: In a shallow roasting pan, combine the olive oil, garlic, tomatoes, shallots, chilies, bell pepper, cumin, coriander, and saffron. Roast in the preheated oven until the tomatoes have darkened in color and begun to brown, about 40 minutes. Meanwhile, put the al-

monds in a food processor fitted with the metal blade and pulse the machine until they are coarsely chopped. In batches, transfer the contents of the pan to the food processor along with batches of basil, parsley, tomato juice, and lime juice. Process until the sauce is smoothly pureed but still slightly coarse. Transfer to a large mixing bowl. Repeat with the remaining batches. Season to taste with salt and pepper.

4. Return half of the sauce to the roasting pan and toss in the rib bones. Loosely cover the pan with foil and cook in the oven for 1 hour. Remove the foil and continue cooking in the oven until the rib bones are browned, about 10 minutes more. Remove from the oven, cover, and keep warm.

5. Raise the oven temperature to 500°F.

6. Remove the lamb from the marinade and pat it dry. Season all over with salt and pepper. Heat a large ovenproof skillet over high heat and add the remaining 3 tablespoons olive oil. Add the lamb and sear until well browned on all sides, 5 to 7 minutes. Spoon the remaining Romesco Sauce over the lamb, put the pan in the oven, and roast until the lamb is done to your liking, about 10 minutes for medium-rare. Remove from the oven, cover loosely with foil, and let the lamb rest for about 10 minutes before carving.

7. To serve, use a sharp knife to cut the lamb crosswise into ½-inch-thick slices. Arrange the slices overlapping on heated serving plates, arrange some roasted rib bones alongside, and spoon over the lamb the hot Romesco Sauce in which the ribs cooked.

Chinois Grilled Lamb Chops
with Cilantro-Mint Vinaigrette

SERVES 4 TO 6

*H*ere's one of the all-time favorites at my Asian fusion restaurant, **Chinois on Main in Santa Monica.** You're probably familiar with the combination of lamb and mint. But adding fresh cilantro and other seasonings from the Far East produces an incredibly delicious new flavor. Look for the best young lamb you can find to get sweet, tender meat that is at its best when quickly cooked medium-rare. Serve with your favorite vegetables and rice, or present the chops alongside mixed baby greens, which also go very well with the vinaigrette.

MARINADE

1 cup soy sauce

1 cup mirin (sweet sake)

1 tablespoon Asian toasted sesame
   oil

2 cups chopped scallions

1 tablespoon dried red chili flakes

2 or 3 garlic cloves, peeled and finely
   chopped

2 racks of lamb, about 2 pounds each,
   trimmed and cut into individual
   chops

Salt

Freshly ground black pepper

CILANTRO-MINT VINAIGRETTE

1/2 cup rice wine vinegar

1/4 cup coarsely chopped fresh mint
   leaves

1/4 cup coarsely chopped fresh
   cilantro leaves

1/4 cup coarsely chopped fresh
   parsley

1 tablespoon honey

1/2 tablespoon chopped ginger

Dash of Asian chili oil

1 cup peanut oil, plus 3 tablespoons
   if sautéing

Salt

Freshly ground black pepper

1. To prepare the marinade: In a bowl, stir together all the marinade ingredients. In a large, shallow, nonreactive dish, pour the marinade over the lamb chops. Cover with plastic wrap and refrigerate for 1 hour

2. While the lamb chops are marinating, prepare the vinaigrette: In a blender, combine all the

ingredients, except the oil and salt and pepper, and blend until smooth. With the machine running, slowly pour in the 1 cup of peanut oil. Season to taste with salt and pepper.

3. Build a fire in an outdoor grill or preheat a gas outdoor or indoor grill, a grill pan, or a broiler. Or heat a skillet over high heat.

4. Remove the lamb chops from the marinade and season them with salt and pepper. Grill or broil them until medium-rare, about 3 minutes per side; or sauté them in the skillet with 3 tablespoons of peanut oil for about 2 minutes per side, cooking the chops in batches if necessary to avoid overcrowding.

5. Spoon some of the vinaigrette on each serving plate and place the lamb chops on top. Spoon more of the vinaigrette over the lamb and serve immediately.

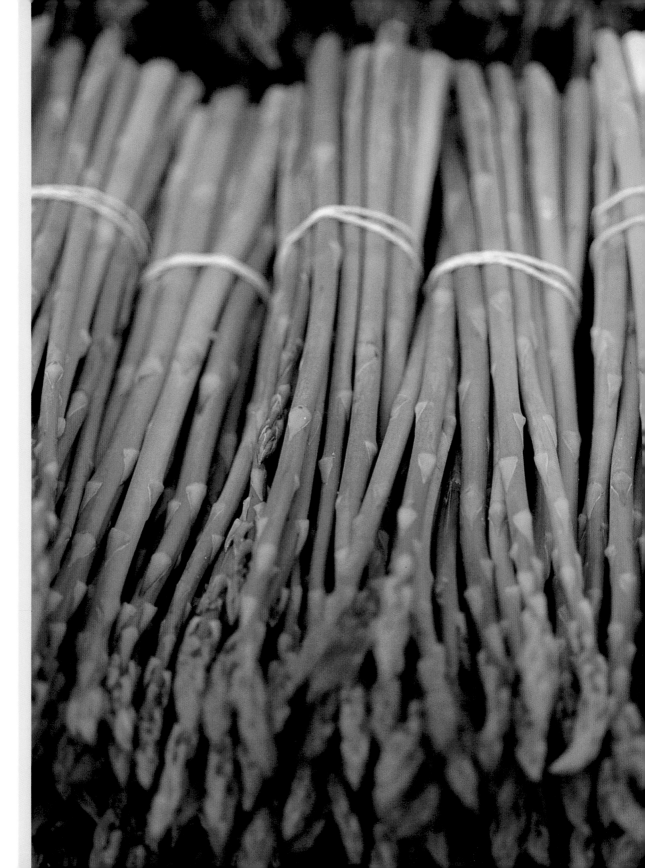

Stir-Fried Vegetables

Dry-Fried String Beans

Zucchini with Basil and Tomatoes

Austrian White Asparagus with Browned Bread Crumbs

Fried Spinach Leaves

Creamy Mashed Potatoes with Caramelized Onions

Roasted-Garlic Mashed Potatoes

Potato Galette with Goat Cheese

Braised Sweet-and-Sour Cabbage

Spaetzle

Braised Chestnuts

Stir-Fried Wild Rice with Apples and Sun-Dried Cherries

Buttermilk Biscuits with Parmesan and Onion

Focaccia

Stir-Fried Vegetables

*T*he combination of the soy sauce, stock, and oil produces a rich brown glaze for the vegetables. When cooked, the vegetables should look shiny and crisp, with no sauce remaining in the pan. Although the list of ingredients looks long, the stir-fry comes together very quickly, so have everything cut up, measured, and lined up by the stove before you start.

1 tablespoon peanut oil

1/4 pound Chinese snow peas, cut into 1-inch pieces

1 cup oyster mushrooms, whole or cut in half, depending upon size

1 cup shiitake mushrooms, whole or cut in half, stems removed (stems can be reserved to add flavor to stocks)

1 cup each red and yellow bell pepper strips, cut into 1-inch chunks

1/2 large Japanese eggplant, cut into 6 or 7 slices

1/4 medium bok choy, cut into 1-inch chunks

5 or 6 broccoli florets

5 young asparagus spears, cut into 1 1/2 to 2-inch lengths

1/3 cup Chicken Stock (page 204) or good-quality canned chicken broth, heated

1 tablespoon soy sauce

Salt

Freshly ground black pepper

1. Heat a wok or a large skillet over high heat. Add the oil. As soon as it is hot, add all the vegetables and, with a large metal stir-frying spatula or wooden spoon, stir-fry them, tossing and stirring continuously to coat the vegetables evenly with the oil.

2. Pour in the stock and the soy sauce and continue stir-frying until the vegetables are al dente, tender but still slightly crisp, about 2 minutes longer. Season with salt and pepper to taste, keeping in mind that the soy sauce is already salty. Serve immediately in a heated serving bowl or arranged attractively on plates as an accompaniment to a main course.

Dry-Fried String Beans

I know so many people who think that dry-fried string beans are their favorite vegetable dish in Chinese restaurants. That makes sense. The quick-cooking technique of deep-frying and then stir-frying the beans gives them a wonderfully crisp texture, deep green color, and fresh flavor, and the sauce ingredients coat them with a rich glaze. I've added my own special touch: some mild-tasting Double-Blanched Garlic, which adds an extra dimension of taste.

1 cup Chicken Stock (page 204) or
    good-quality canned chicken broth
1/4 cup bottled oyster sauce
1/4 cup soy sauce
1/4 cup sugar
3 tablespoons peanut oil, plus 4 cups
    for deep-frying

1 cup Double-Blanched Garlic
    (page 220)
1 pound haricots verts (French-style
    thin green beans), stems removed,
    rinsed and patted thoroughly dry
Thai basil leaves or thinly sliced
    scallions, for garnish

1. In a small bowl, stir together the stock, oyster sauce, soy sauce, and sugar.

2. In a medium sauté pan or wok over medium heat, heat the 3 tablespoons of oil. Add the garlic cloves and cook them, stirring frequently, until they caramelize to a golden-brown color, 7 to 10 minutes. Add 1 cup of the sauce mixture and continue cooking, stirring frequently, until it reduces to a glaze that coats the garlic, about 10 minutes more. Set aside.

3. In a deep-fryer or heavy-bottomed pot, heat the 4 cups of peanut oil to 375°F on a deep-frying thermometer. Add the string beans and fry them for about 20 seconds. Using a wire skimmer or slotted spoon, remove the beans from the oil and drain on paper towels.

4. Add the beans and remaining sauce to the wok or skillet with the garlic. Toss over medium heat just until the beans are well coated. Transfer to a heated serving plate or bowl and garnish with Thai basil or scallions. Serve immediately.

Zucchini with Basil and Tomatoes

*C*ome summer, ask anybody with a cultivated plot of land how their garden grows and they'll probably tell you it's overrun with zucchini. Here's a great, easy recipe for using them up, even if you buy them at the market. Choose zucchini that are small and firm, and only vine-ripened, juicy tomatoes. Fresh basil provides the perfect aromatic finishing touch. The mixture is also good cold, like a very basic ratatouille.

12 to 15 baby zucchini (about 1 pound), trimmed

2 tablespoons extra-virgin olive oil

2 garlic cloves, peeled and minced

3 ripe medium tomatoes, peeled, seeded, diced, and drained (page 217)

1 cup julienned fresh basil leaves (page 229)

Salt

Freshly ground pepper

1. Cut the zucchini diagonally into ¼-inch-thick slices, or into ¼-inch cubes.

2. In a large skillet, heat the olive oil over high heat. Add the zucchini and garlic and sauté, stirring frequently, for 2 minutes. Add the tomatoes and basil and continue to cook, stirring occasionally, until the zucchini are tender, about 3 minutes more.

3. Season to taste with salt and pepper. Serve in a heated serving bowl or arrange attractively on each plate as an accompaniment to a main course.

Austrian White Asparagus
with Browned Bread Crumbs

SERVES 2 TO 4

*J*ulia Child loved this dish when I cooked it for her on my Food Network TV show. Like Julia, many people prize white asparagus, stalks that are "blanched" by growing them in dirt-covered mounds to deprive them of sunlight and stop their chlorophyll from developing. They have a very delicate flavor, which makes a nice counterpoint to their plump size and robust texture. However, you can also make this with jumbo green asparagus. Cook the large spears long enough to make them tender and juicy. Topping them with bread crumbs browned in butter is a classic Austrian touch that also works well with other vegetables like broccoli or cauliflower. Serve the asparagus as a side dish with poultry or meat, or offer it as a special appetizer.

12 white asparagus spears

Salt

1/4 pound (1 stick) unsalted butter

1 cup brioche crumbs or other good-quality white or egg bread crumbs

1 teaspoon minced fresh parsley leaves

Freshly ground black pepper

1. On a cutting board, line the asparagus up with their tips even. Measuring from the tips, cut off their ends to give them uniform 6-inch lengths. Starting 1½ to 2 inches below the tip, peel off their tough skins with a vegetable peeler.

2. In a medium saucepan, bring salted water to a boil. Cook the asparagus for 10 to 12 minutes, until the spears are tender enough to be pierced easily with the tip of a small, sharp knife. Take care not to overcook them. Drain the asparagus, pat them dry with paper towels, and set them aside.

3. In a large sauté pan over medium heat, melt the butter. Add the brioche crumbs or bread crumbs and sauté until golden, about 5 minutes. Add the asparagus spears and turn them in the bread crumbs and butter until they are well coated, adding the parsley and seasoning with a little salt and pepper to taste during the final moments. Transfer the asparagus to a heated serving platter, spoon any crumbs remaining in the pan over them, and serve immediately.

Fried Spinach Leaves

*O*ne of the prettiest vegetable side dishes or garnishes I know, deep-fried spinach leaves have a deep green color and a shimmering translucency. Even if you aren't a spinach fan, you'll love the way these taste. I could almost eat them as a snack, they're so good. You can also use this basic technique to deep-fry fresh herbs as a garnish; basil, sage, and flat-leaf parsley work especially well. Whatever kind of leaves you use, make sure they are absolutely dry before immersing them in the oil, to avoid splattering.

Peanut oil for deep-frying

1/2 pound baby spinach leaves, thoroughly trimmed, rinsed, and patted dry with paper towels

Kosher salt

1. In a wok, deep-fryer, or deep, heavy saucepan, heat about 3 inches of peanut oil to 375°F on a deep-frying thermometer.

2. Add the spinach leaves to the hot oil, using a wire skimmer or slotted spoon to immerse them completely. Fry until crisp and translucent, 1 to 2 minutes. Remove them with the skimmer or slotted spoon and transfer to paper towels to drain. Season to taste with salt and serve immediately.

Creamy Mashed Potatoes with Caramelized Onions

*I*f I had to choose my favorite topping for mashed potatoes, it would be shaved white truffles. But onions sautéed until their natural sugars caramelize are delicious, adding flavor, texture, and deep golden-brown color to the potatoes. You can also sprinkle the onions over pizza, pasta, burgers, steaks, or meat loaf. If you make the onions for this recipe in advance, gently reheat them in a nonstick skillet before topping the potatoes.

CARAMELIZED ONIONS

2 tablespoons extra-virgin olive oil

1 large red, yellow, or white onion
(about 3/4 pound), peeled, trimmed,
and cut into 3/4-inch pieces

2 tablespoons balsamic vinegar

Kosher salt

Freshly ground black pepper

CREAMY MASHED POTATOES

2 1/2 pounds baking potatoes, peeled
and cut into even 1 1/2- to 2 1/2-inch
chunks

Salt

1/2 cup heavy cream, brought to a boil

1/4 pound (1 stick) unsalted butter, cut
into small pieces, at room
temperature

Freshly ground white pepper

Freshly grated nutmeg

1 tablespoon chopped fresh parsley

1. To make the Caramelized Onions: In a 10-inch skillet over medium heat, heat the oil. Add the onion and cook, stirring frequently, until lightly browned, about 15 minutes. Stir in the

vinegar and cook 1 minute longer. Season to taste with salt and pepper. If not using the onion immediately, let it cool to room temperature, transfer it to a covered container, and store in the refrigerator for up to 3 to 5 days.

2. To make the Creamy Mashed Potatoes: Put the potatoes in a saucepan filled with enough lightly salted cold water to cover them well. Bring the water to a boil over high heat, then reduce the heat slightly and simmer briskly until the potatoes are fork-tender, 15 to 20 minutes.

3. Meanwhile, put the cream in a small saucepan and heat it over low heat.

4. When the potatoes are done, drain them well. Pass the potatoes through a food mill set over the saucepan, or put them back in the pan and mash them with a potato masher until they are as smooth as you like them.

5. Add the butter and warm cream to the mashed potatoes and stir over low heat with a wooden spoon until thoroughly blended in. Season the potatoes to taste with salt, pepper, and just a little nutmeg.

6. Spoon the mashed potatoes onto warmed serving plates or into a warmed serving bowl and garnish with the Caramelized Onions and the parsley. Serve immediately.

Roasted-Garlic Mashed Potatoes

SERVES 6 TO 8

*I*f you like fluffy mashed potatoes and you like garlic, then you'll love this dish. The difference between this version and the usual garlic mashed potato recipes you find lies in its use of oven-roasted garlic, which gives the potatoes a mellow, sweet garlic flavor worlds away from what you might expect.

2^1/$_2$ pounds baking potatoes, peeled
 and cut into even 1^1/$_2$- to 2-inch
 chunks

Salt

^{1}/$_4$ pound (1 stick) unsalted butter, cut
 into small pieces, at room
 temperature

^{1}/$_2$ cup heavy cream

^{1}/$_2$ cup Roasted Whole Garlic puree
 (page 219)

Freshly ground white pepper

Freshly grated nutmeg

1 tablespoon chopped fresh parsley,
 for garnish

1. Put the potatoes in a saucepan filled with enough lightly salted cold water to cover them well. Bring the water to a boil over high heat, then reduce the heat slightly and simmer briskly until the potatoes are fork-tender, 15 to 20 minutes. Drain well. Pass the potatoes through a food mill set over the saucepan, or put them back in the pan and mash them with a potato masher until they are as smooth as you like them.

2. In a small saucepan over medium-low heat, heat the butter and cream until the butter has melted. Add the butter-cream mixture and roasted garlic to the potatoes and stir or mash until fully incorporated. Season to taste with salt, pepper, and nutmeg. Spoon the mashed potatoes into a warmed serving bowl or onto individual plates and sprinkle with chopped parsley. Serve immediately.

Potato Galette with Goat Cheese

SERVES 4

A perfect accompaniment for red meat or poultry, especially generously spiced dishes, this French-style potato cake also makes an impressive vegetarian main course, accompanied by a mixed green salad. Or you could top it with smoked salmon for a very special appetizer. Be sure you cook the first layer of potatoes long enough so they stick together, which will keep the cheese from leaking out the bottom. To clarify the butter for this recipe, melt about 1/2 cup (1/4 pound) unsalted butter in a small saucepan over low heat. Let the solids settle to the bottom of the pan; then, carefully pour off the clear butter from the top into a clean container, stopping before any milky solids pour out. Store any excess clarified butter covered in the refrigerator for up to several weeks.

1 pound baking potatoes, peeled,
   thinly sliced

1/4 cup clarified butter

Salt

2 ounces shredded mozzarella cheese

2 ounces fresh goat cheese

1. Preheat the oven to 450°F.

2. Put the potato slices in a medium bowl, pour the clarified butter over them, season lightly with salt, and toss to coat the slices evenly.

3. Arrange half the potatoes, overlapping like a flower, in a 9-inch ovenproof skillet, preferably nonstick. Cook over medium heat until the edges begin to brown and the potatoes stick together, about 10 minutes. Sprinkle evenly with the mozzarella and dot with the goat cheese, then cover with the remaining potatoes in a similar pattern.

4. Transfer the skillet to the oven and bake for 10 minutes. Remove the skillet from the oven and invert a large heatproof plate over it; carefully holding the plate and skillet together with oven gloves or pot holders, flip them over to unmold the galette onto the plate. Then slide the galette from the plate back into the pan and continue to cook on the stovetop over medium-high heat until the underside is nicely browned, 5 to 7 minutes more. Return the skillet to the oven to finish cooking for about 5 minutes more.

5. To serve the galette, slide it out of the skillet onto a cutting board. With a large, sharp knife, cut it into quarters. Transfer them to a heated platter or individual serving plates.

Braised Sweet-and-Sour Cabbage

SERVES 12

I like to serve this old family recipe at large gatherings, especially during the holiday season. The combination of robust cabbage and sweet and sour seasonings goes great with pork, ham, beef, and other festive roasts. You can store any leftovers in the refrigerator in a covered, nonreactive container for 2 or 3 days, and reheat them for another meal.

1/4 cup peanut oil or vegetable oil

1 medium red onion, peeled and sliced

1 cup light brown sugar

2 Granny Smith apples, cored and sliced

1/2 cup red wine vinegar

2 cups red wine

2 cups orange juice

1 cinnamon stick

1 teaspoon ground ginger

Salt

Freshly ground black pepper

4 pounds red cabbage, quartered, cored, cut into wedges, and cut crosswise into thin strips

1. Preheat the oven to 350°F.

2. Heat a heavy casserole over medium-high heat. Add the oil and the red onion and sauté until the onion turns translucent, about 3 minutes. Sprinkle in the brown sugar and continue sautéing, stirring frequently, until the onion starts to caramelize, about 5 minutes.

3. Add the apples, pour in the red wine vinegar, and stir and scrape with a wooden spoon to deglaze the pan. Add the red wine, orange juice, cinnamon stick, ginger, and salt and pepper to taste. Bring the liquid to a boil, reduce the heat, and simmer for 5 minutes.

4. Stir in the cabbage and cook for about 10 minutes on top of the stove. Cover the casserole with its lid or aluminum foil, transfer to the oven, and continue cooking until the cabbage is tender, about 45 minutes. Remove the casserole from the oven, remove and discard the cinnamon stick, taste the cabbage, and adjust the seasoning if necessary.

Spaetzle

*D*id you know that the Austrian word for these little handmade egg-and-flour dumplings actually means "little sparrows"? I guess some of the pointy shapes look a bit like birds, and, correctly made, they can be wonderfully light, though I'm not sure you'd call them light as a feather. Anyway, I grew up eating more spaetzle than noodles. Once you've tasted this version, you'll be hooked. They're the traditional companion to goulash (page 134). But I'd be happy eating them as a side dish with any hearty meat or poultry main course, or just on their own as a simple meal.

4 egg yolks

1 egg

1³/₄ cups milk

About 3 cups all-purpose flour

    (1 pound)

1 teaspoon salt, plus more to taste

¹/₄ teaspoon freshly ground black

    pepper, plus more to taste

¹/₄ teaspoon freshly grated nutmeg

¹/₄ pound (1 stick) unsalted butter,

    melted

¹/₂ cup peanut oil or vegetable oil

4 tablespoons (¹/₂ stick) unsalted

    butter, cut into pieces

1 tablespoon minced fresh parsley

1. In a small bowl, use a fork to beat together the egg yolks, egg, and milk.

2. In a medium mixing bowl, stir together the flour, 1 teaspoon of salt, ¼ teaspoon of pepper, and nutmeg. Add the melted butter and the egg mixture and mix with your hands just until well blended; take care not to overmix the batter. Cover the bowl with plastic wrap and refrigerate to rest and chill for at least 1 hour.

3. Bring a large pot of salted water to a boil. Fill a mixing bowl with ice and water and place it on the counter near the sink. Place a large-holed colander on top of the pot. Spoon the batter into the colander. With a large wooden spoon, press and force the batter through the holes in the colander, moving the spoon back and forth across the holes to help break off the bits of dough. Occasionally scrape any batter clinging to the underside, letting it drop into the water. Boil the spaetzle until they have risen to the surface and are cooked through but still a little chewy, 4 to 5 minutes.

4. Drain the spaetzle, then immediately transfer them to the bowl of ice water to arrest the cooking. When the spaetzle are cool to the touch, drain them again thoroughly. Return them to a clean bowl and toss them gently with ¼ cup of the oil. (At this point, you may cover the bowl with plastic wrap and refrigerate up to 2 days.)

5. When you are ready to serve the spaetzle, heat a large sauté pan over high heat until it is very hot. Add the remaining ¼ cup oil and the boiled spaetzle. Let them cook undisturbed, without moving the pan, until their undersides begin to turn golden brown, about 2 minutes. Reduce the heat slightly, add the pieces of butter, and sauté the spaetzle, stirring continuously but gently, until they are uniformly golden brown, 3 to 4 minutes more. Season to taste with salt and pepper. Finish with a sprinkle of parsley.

Braised Chestnuts

*T*hey may not be roasted on an open fire, but these chestnuts still can help to make any holiday meal brighter. Peel the chestnuts a few hours ahead of time if you like. If you don't want to go through the trouble of peeling them yourself, you can sometimes find cans of whole peeled chestnuts in well-stocked markets.

2 pounds whole chestnuts

2 tablespoons vegetable oil

2 tablespoons unsalted butter

1/2 cup finely chopped onion

1 cup port

3 cups Chicken Stock (page 204) or good-quality canned chicken broth

1 sprig of fresh thyme

Salt

Freshly ground black pepper

1. First, peel the chestnuts: Bring a large pot of water to a boil. Meanwhile, carefully use the tip of a small, sharp knife to cut a shallow *X* through the skin on the flat side of each chestnut. Put the chestnuts in the boiling water and boil them for about 15 minutes. Drain the chestnuts, return them to the emptied pot, and put on the lid; turn off the stove and place the covered pot on an unlit burner to keep the nuts warm. Remove the chestnuts a few at a time from the pot with a folded

kitchen towel. With your fingers or, if necessary, the knife, carefully peel away the skin starting at the corners of the X, removing the beige inner skin as well.

2. Heat a heavy saucepan over medium-high heat. Add the oil, butter, and chopped onion and sauté until the onions are lightly browned, about 5 minutes. Add the port and stir and scrape to dissolve the pan deposits. Add the peeled chestnuts, the Chicken Stock, thyme, and a little salt and pepper to taste. Cover and cook until the chestnuts are tender and have absorbed most of the liquid, 30 to 45 minutes.

3. Transfer the chestnuts to a warmed serving dish. Or, to make a wonderful chestnut puree, press them hot through a ricer and enrich by stirring in a little butter or warmed cream.

Stir-Fried Wild Rice with Apples and Sun-Dried Cherries

SERVES 2

The cooking method will probably remind you of Asian fried rice. But this combination of nutty-tasting wild rice, actually the grains of a grass native to the Great Lakes, and fresh and dried fruit is all-American. (Okay, so the curry powder adds an exotic touch, but it goes really well with the onion and the sweet and tangy fruit flavors.) Offer this next to your favorite holiday main course, or at any time of year. You can precook the wild rice a day or two in advance and keep it covered and refrigerated before going ahead with the rest of the recipe. Double or triple the quantities if you like.

1/2 cup uncooked wild rice

1 1/2 cups cold water

2 tablespoons extra-virgin olive oil

2 tablespoons minced onion

1 tablespoon curry powder

1 apple, peeled, cored, and cut into
small dice

1 cup coarsely chopped mushrooms

1/4 cup sun-dried cherries

Salt

Freshly ground black pepper

1. First, cook the wild rice: In a sieve, rinse the rice under cold running water, then drain well. Put the rice and cold water in a small saucepan. Bring the water to a boil and stir the rice briefly; reduce the heat to very low, cover the pan, and simmer until the rice is tender, 35 to 45 minutes. Check the water level toward the end of cooking and, if necessary, add a little more boiling water. Remove the pan from the heat and let it stand, covered, for about 10 minutes more. You will have about 1½ cups.

2. Heat a sauté pan over medium heat. Add the olive oil and onion and sauté until the onion is translucent, 2 to 3 minutes. Stir in the curry powder and sauté briefly, just until its aroma develops. Stir in the apple, mushrooms, and sun-dried cherries and continue sautéing, stirring continuously, until the mushrooms are cooked through, 2 to 3 minutes more.

3. Add the cooked wild rice and sauté, stirring continuously, just until it is heated through and well mixed with the other ingredients. Season to taste with salt and pepper and serve immediately.

Buttermilk Biscuits with Parmesan and Onion

MAKES 20 TO 22 BISCUITS

*C*rusty on the outside and light and buttery inside, these biscuits are so quick and easy to make that they could become a regular item at your weekend table. Once you've had them a few times, feel free to start playing with the recipe. You might want to add some finely chopped jalapeño or toasted sesame seeds. Or, in place of the cheese and onion, try plumped raisins for a sweeter biscuit. Serve them with morning eggs, with a bowl of soup or stew, or with shaved country ham.

2³/4 cups all-purpose flour

1¹/2 tablespoons sugar

1 tablespoon plus 1 teaspoon baking powder

2 teaspoons salt

¹/4 teaspoon baking soda

10 tablespoons chilled unsalted butter, cut into small pieces

¹/4 cup minced onion

1 tablespoon chopped fresh thyme or 2 teaspoons dried thyme

1 cup buttermilk

1 to 2 tablespoons milk or cream

¹/4 cup grated Parmesan cheese

1. In a food processor fitted with the metal blade, combine the flour, sugar, baking powder, salt, and baking soda. Add the butter, onion, and thyme, and process until the mixture resembles fine meal. With the machine running, pour the buttermilk through the feed tube, just until the dough comes together.

2. Turn out the dough onto a well-floured work surface and knead lightly into a round ball.

Roll out the dough to a 1-inch thickness. With a 2-inch round cutter, cut out as many biscuits as you can, transferring them to two parchment paper–lined baking sheets. Gather up the dough, lightly knead it together, and repeat the rolling out and cutting process until you have used all the dough, giving you 20 to 22 biscuits. Cover with plastic wrap and refrigerate for at least 1 hour or up to 24 hours.

3.   Preheat the oven to 350°F.

4.   Uncover the baking sheets. Lightly brush the top of each biscuit with milk or cream and sprinkle with the Parmesan cheese. Bake the biscuits until lightly golden brown, 25 to 35 minutes. Serve hot or warm.

Focaccia

*T*he popular Italian yeast-leavened flatbread is really nothing more than a pizza dough baked in thin sheets brushed with olive oil and seasonings instead of with sauce, cheese, and toppings. In place of the pepper and fresh thyme in this recipe, try topping the bread with fresh rosemary leaves, thinly sliced onions or shallots, chopped garlic, chili oil, a sprinkling of freshly grated Parmesan cheese, or anything else that sounds good to you. I've even had incredible focaccia studded with whole red seedless grapes and sprinkled with rosemary. Serve squares of your focaccia with soup, salad, pasta, or a main dish; or use it as it comes or split in half to make sensational sandwiches. I think an electric stand mixer is ideal for making bread; you can also use a food processor, following the manufacturer's instructions for mixing and kneading the dough.

$1/2$ cup extra-virgin olive oil, plus
   more for brushing

1 package active dry yeast

$13/4$ cups warm (105°F to 115°F) water

1 tablespoon honey

$11/2$ pounds bread flour

1 tablespoon kosher salt, plus more
   for sprinkling

Freshly ground black pepper

Fresh thyme leaves, minced

1. Brush a 15 by 11-inch baking sheet with olive oil and set aside.

2. In a measuring cup or bowl of a stand mixer, combine the yeast, ½ cup of the water, and the honey. Stir by hand until the yeast dissolves. Stir in ¼ cup of the flour to make a sponge. Cover the bowl with plastic wrap and leave at warm room temperature to rise until doubled in volume, 1 to 2 hours.

3. In the stand mixer bowl, combine the risen sponge with the remaining flour, water, olive oil, and the salt. Using the dough hook attachment, mix at medium speed until a soft dough forms. Continue beating for 2 minutes. Turn off the machine, scrape down the sides of the bowl, and leave the dough to relax for 10 minutes.

4. Turn the mixer back on at medium speed and continue to mix the dough until it becomes velvety and elastic, about 5 minutes more.

5. Transfer the dough to the prepared baking sheet. With your hands, stretch, push, and pull it out to fill the baking sheet evenly. Cover the dough loosely with clean kitchen towels and leave it to rise at room temperature for about 20 minutes.

6. Uncover the dough and stretch it out again to fill the entire baking sheet to its rim. Brush the dough with olive oil and press your fingertips down into it at regular intervals to dimple it. Sprinkle generously to taste with kosher salt, pepper, and thyme. Leave the dough to rise for 15 minutes. Meanwhile, preheat the oven to 400°F.

7. Put the baking sheet in the oven and bake the focaccia for 10 minutes. Rotate the tray and continue baking until the bread is golden brown and well risen, 6 to 8 minutes more. Serve hot, warm, or at room temperature, cut into squares.

Wolfgang's Tarte Tatin

Baked Apple Pouches with Cinnamon and Raisins

Decadent Warm Chocolate Cupcakes with Molten Centers

My Favorite Chocolate Cake

Chocolate Shortbread Footballs

Raspberries in Puff Pastry

Caramelized Lemon-Lime Torte

Cookies-and-Cream Cheesecake

Classic Spago Cheesecake

Kaiserschmarren

Salzburger Nockerln with Fresh Raspberry Jam

White Chocolate Malt Ice Cream

Almond Granita

Melon Granita

Wolfgang's Tarte Tatin

*T*here are many versions of the classic French apple tarte Tatin, a caramelized apple tart baked upside down and supposedly invented by two French innkeeper sisters named Tatin. I hope they'd approve of my version, which takes a little liberty with the original. I like to use Puff Pastry and to cook the apples separately so the fruit comes out perfectly while the crust stays light and crisp right up to the time you serve it. For a shortcut, look for ready-to-use puff pastry dough in your supermarket's freezer case.

<table>
<tr><td>1/4 pound (1 stick) unsalted butter</td><td>1 1/2 cups sugar</td></tr>
<tr><td>12 medium Golden Delicious apples,</td><td>1/2 pound Puff Pastry (page 213)</td></tr>
<tr><td>   peeled, cored, and quartered</td><td>Whipped cream or vanilla ice cream</td></tr>
</table>

1. Preheat the oven to 450°F.
2. Using half the butter, heavily grease the bottom and sides of a 10 by 3-inch round cake pan. Arrange the apple quarters in the pan in a continuous sunburst pattern, with the ends of the quarters pointing toward the center and the side, placing the first layer of quarters with their rounded sides down; place the remaining pieces rounded sides

up, fitting them neatly among the other quarters. Evenly sprinkle 1 cup of the sugar over the apples and dot them evenly with the remaining butter.

3. Bake the apples in the preheated oven for 30 minutes. Reduce the oven temperature to 350°F and continue to bake until the apples are soft and a deep caramel brown on top, about 1 hour longer.

4. While the apples are baking, prepare the crust. Roll out the Puff Pastry to form a 12-inch square about ⅛ inch thick. Place the pastry on a lightly greased baking sheet. Using another 10-inch baking pan or plate as a guide, cut out a circle slightly larger than 10 inches in diameter, removing and discarding the trimmings. With the tines of a fork, evenly prick the pastry all over to help it rise evenly during baking. Bake the pastry in the 350°F oven with the apples until golden brown, 25 to 35 minutes. When both the apples and the pastry are done, remove them from the oven and let them cool completely to room temperature.

5. To assemble the tart, preheat the broiler. Transfer the pastry to a serving platter and, carefully holding the platter and pastry together, invert them over the pan of apples, aligning them neatly. Securely hold together the pan and platter with both hands and invert them again. Carefully lift off the inverted cake pan to unmold the apples onto the pastry, neatly replacing any apples that come dislodged or stick to the pan. Sprinkle the remaining sugar evenly over the apples and broil 3 to 4 inches from the heat just until the sugar caramelizes, 1 to 2 minutes. Cut the tart into wedges and serve with whipped cream or ice cream.

Baked Apple Pouches with Cinnamon and Raisins

I love baseball. **A visit to Dodger Stadium for my Food Network television show inspired me to come up with this ball-shaped version of a dessert that's literally as American as apple pie. The apple pouches are so easy to make because the pastry is ready-to-use egg roll skins that you can find in the refrigerated case of big supermarkets. They bake up wonderfully delicate and crisp. Serve these to your guests and you'll hit a home run. You'll need some good cotton or linen kitchen string for keeping the pouches tied shut while they bake.**

7 tablespoons unsalted butter

1 pound Granny Smith apples, peeled, cored, and thinly sliced

1/4 cup sugar

1/4 cup golden raisins

Juice of 1 lemon

1/2 teaspoon ground cinnamon

1 package large square egg roll skins

Confectioners' sugar, for garnish

Vanilla ice cream

1. Preheat the oven to 350°F. Line a baking sheet with parchment paper and set it aside. Cut 8 pieces of kitchen string, each 6 to 8 inches long, and set aside.

2. In a large sauté pan over medium heat, melt the butter; pour off 1/4 cup of the melted butter and set it aside. Add the apples, sugar, raisins, lemon juice, and cinnamon to the pan and sauté, stirring frequently, until the apples are tender, about 8 minutes. Remove from the heat.

3. Place an egg roll skin on a flat work surface with one of its corners pointing to you. Place another egg roll skin on top, perfectly aligned with the first. Spoon 1/4 cup of the filling into the center of the wrappers and gather the corners up around the filling to create a pouch. With a piece of kitchen string, tie the corners securely together to completely enclose the filling, but don't tie the string too tight. Transfer the pouch to the baking sheet. Repeat with the rest of the ingredients to make 8 pouches in all.

4. Brush the pouches with the reserved melted butter. Put the baking sheet in the oven and bake the pouches until their wrappers are golden brown and crisp, 10 to 15 minutes.

5. Transfer the pouches to individual serving plates and, using kitchen scissors or the tip of a small sharp knife, carefully snip off their strings. Holding a small, fine-meshed sieve over the pouches, spoon into it some confectioners' sugar, then tap the sieve to dust the sugar over each pouch. Place a scoop of vanilla ice cream alongside each serving.

Decadent Warm Chocolate Cupcakes with Molten Centers

SERVES 6

.. **D**efinitely not your usual cupcakes, these bake in ramekins or individual custard cups and come to the table still warm, their centers gooey and seductive. The room will go quiet when you serve them, followed by a chorus of soft, satisfied moans. For an extra decorative touch, as shown here, garnish each serving with chocolate shavings.

12 tablespoons (1½ sticks) unsalted butter

5 ounces bittersweet chocolate, broken into pieces

3 large eggs

3 large egg yolks

¼ cup sugar

3 tablespoons all-purpose flour

Lightly sweetened whipped cream or vanilla ice cream

1. Preheat the oven to 350°F. Melt 2 tablespoons of the butter in a small saucepan or a microwave-proof dish and evenly brush it inside six 8-ounce custard cups or ramekins.

2. In the top of a double boiler or in a medium heat-proof bowl set over barely simmering water, melt the chocolate and remaining butter together. Remove from the heat.

3. In the large bowl of an electric mixer, or in a large

mixing bowl using a handheld electric mixer, beat together the eggs, egg yolks, and sugar at medium speed until the mixture is pale yellow, thick, and creamy, about 5 minutes.

4. Using a rubber spatula, fold about one third of the egg mixture at a time into the melted chocolate-butter mixture. When they are fully incorporated, evenly sprinkle and gently fold in the flour until no streaks remain. Pour the batter into the prepared cups or ramekins, filling them about two thirds full.

5. Place the cups or ramekins on a baking sheet and bake until the sides of the cupcakes look firm but their centers are still moist when a wooden toothpick is inserted into the center of one, 10 to 12 minutes. Remove the cupcakes from the oven and set them aside to cool for about 10 minutes before serving, either in their cups or ramekins or unmolded onto serving plates. Serve with lightly sweetened whipped cream or vanilla ice cream.

My Favorite Chocolate Cake

SERVES 8 TO 12

.. *I* love the simple things in life—like this flourless chocolate cake, which is made with just a few ingredients and tastes amazing. For the best results, start with the finest-quality chocolate you can find.

8 ounces bittersweet chocolate,
    broken into small pieces

1/4 pound (1 stick) unsalted butter, cut
    into small pieces

5 large eggs, separated

2/3 cup sugar

Pinch of salt

Confectioners' sugar, for garnish

Unsweetened whipped cream,
    for garnish

Fresh berries, for garnish

1. Preheat the oven to 325°F. Butter and flour a 10-inch round cake pan and line its bottom with a piece of parchment paper, using the pan as a guide to cut out the paper.

2. Bring a pan of water or the bottom of a double boiler to a boil. Reduce the heat to maintain a bare simmer. In the top half of the double boiler, or in a heatproof bowl set over but not touching the water, melt the chocolate and butter together, stirring occasionally. Set the chocolate-butter mixture aside.

3. In a mixing bowl, put the egg yolks and all but 3 tablespoons of the sugar. Whisk them until the sugar has dissolved and the yolks are smooth. Whisking continuously, slowly pour in the melted chocolate until thoroughly combined.

4. Put the egg whites and salt in a clean bowl. With an electric mixer on medium speed, beat the egg whites until soft peaks form when the beaters are lifted out. Gradually sprinkle and beat in the remaining sugar and continue to beat until the egg whites form stiff but not dry-looking peaks when the beaters are lifted out.

5. Stir a dollop of the egg whites into the chocolate mixture to lighten it. Then, a third at a time, gently fold the chocolate mixture into the egg whites just until thoroughly combined. Pour the mixture into the prepared cake pan.

6. Bake the cake until it looks firm and set but a wooden toothpick inserted into the center stills comes out slightly moist, about 45 minutes. Immediately turn the cake out onto a

cooling rack by using potholders or oven gloves to hold the rack securely on top of the pan and then inverting them together and lifting off the pan. Peel off the parchment paper. As the cake cools, its center will sink and crack, but do not worry.

7. Before serving, put some confectioners' sugar in a fine-meshed sieve held over the cake, and tap the sieve to dust the cake with sugar. Cut the cake into wedges and serve with unsweetened whipped cream or berries.

Chocolate Shortbread Footballs

MAKES 1 DOZEN SANDWICH COOKIES

I wouldn't call myself a football fanatic. But I do love the idea of tailgate parties, not to mention the huge spreads of good food people assemble on coffee tables to enjoy together while they watch the big game. Let me add these fun cookies to the menu. They have an intense chocolate flavor, a buttery shortbread crispness, and the unexpected tang of mascarpone, Italy's thick soured cream cheese, in the filling.

Since the cookies have an icing that includes uncooked egg whites, I want to pass along this advisory from the **American Egg Board**: "There have been warnings against consuming raw or lightly cooked eggs on the grounds that the egg may be contaminated with **Salmonella**, a bacteria responsible for a type of food poisoning. Healthy people need to remember that there is a very small risk and to treat eggs and other raw animal foods accordingly. Use only properly refrigerated, clean, sound-shelled, fresh, grade **AA** or **A** eggs. Avoid mixing yolks and whites with their shell."

COOKIES

1/2 pound (2 sticks) unsalted butter

1/2 cup granulated sugar

1 1/2 cups sifted all-purpose flour

3/4 cup sifted unsweetened cocoa
　　powder

FILLING

1 cup mascarpone

2 tablespoons confectioners' sugar

ROYAL ICING

1 cup sifted confectioners' sugar

1 tablespoon egg white

1.　Put the butter and sugar in a mixing bowl. With an electric mixer on medium speed, cream them together for 5 minutes. Add the flour and cocoa powder and beat until thoroughly combined. Cover the bowl with plastic wrap and refrigerate for 1 hour.

2. Preheat the oven to 350°F. Line a baking sheet with parchment paper.

3. On a flat, smooth work surface lightly dusted with flour, gather the dough together in a ball and, with a lightly flour-dusted rolling pin, roll the dough out to an even ¼-inch thickness. With a football-shaped cookie cutter about 3 inches long, cut the dough into 2 dozen football shapes. (Alternatively, draw a similarly sized football freehand on a piece of cardboard and cut it out with scissors. Then, use the cardboard as a template, placing it on top of the dough and carefully cutting around its contours with the tip of a small, sharp knife.) Transfer the cookies to the paper-lined baking sheet. Bake

for 10 minutes. Rotate the sheet 180 degrees and bake another 5 minutes. Remove the sheet from the oven, transfer the cookies to a wire rack, and let them cool.

4. In a mixing bowl, stir together the mascarpone and the 2 tablespoons of confectioners' sugar until well blended. Spread a little of this mixture on top of one football and top with a second football to make a sandwich. Continue spreading the mixture until all cookies are filled.

5. To make the Royal Icing, in a clean bowl stir together the 1 cup of confectioners' sugar and the egg white until perfectly smooth. Spoon the icing into a piping bag fitted with a round number-1 tip, or spoon it into a sealable plastic bag. Using the tip, or snipping off the very tip of one corner of the plastic bag with scissors to form an opening, pipe a football lace design on the cookies. Let the icing dry before serving.

Raspberries in Puff Pastry

You won't believe how easy it is to make a dessert that looks and tastes so elegant and delicious. You can prepare the different parts of the recipe earlier in the day and just put them together moments before you serve them. (Or take the shortcut of buying premade, ready-to-bake puff pastry from your supermarket's freezer case.) The baked puff pastry squares, called feuilletées, can also be used with other fillings—different fruits or your favorite ice cream and other sweet sauces.

1/2 pound **Puff Pastry** (page 213)

1 egg lightly beaten with 1 tablespoon of water

1 cup heavy cream, whipped

2 tablespoons **Grand Marnier** or other orange-flavored liqueur

3 cups fresh raspberries

1. Preheat the oven to 450°F.

2. Roll out the Puff Pastry to a rectangle slightly larger than 6 by 9 inches and about ⅜ inch thick. Cut the pastry into six 3-inch squares. Transfer the squares to a baking sheet and brush them with the beaten egg, being careful not to let any egg drip onto the baking sheet. Bake for 5 minutes, then reduce the heat to 350°F and bake until the pastry is well puffed and golden brown, about 20 minutes longer.

3. Meanwhile, in a mixing bowl, whisk together the whipped cream and Grand Marnier. Cover with plastic wrap and refrigerate until needed.

4. When the pastry squares are done, transfer them to a wire rack to cool. With a sharp, serrated knife, carefully slice each one horizontally in half.

5. To assemble, place the bottom half of each pastry on a dessert plate and spread it with a large dollop of the whipped cream mixture. Arrange the berries on top of the whipped cream and place the other half of the pastry on top, slightly angled to reveal the filling. Serve immediately.

Caramelized Lemon-Lime Tart

.. $\mathcal{I}$ know several big **Hollywood** stars who always seemed to come to the old **Spago Hollywood** just to eat this wonderful rich and tangy dessert. Together, the fresh lemon and lime juices and zests give it a flavor tantalizingly in between a classic lemon curd tart and a key lime pie, while the caramelized topping adds the special appeal of a crème brûlée. **How often do you get three desserts in one?**

1/2 recipe Sugar Dough (page 216)

4 whole eggs

4 egg yolks

1 cup plus 2 tablespoons sugar

2/3 cup lemon juice

2/3 cup lime juice

Grated zest of 2 small lemons

Grated zest of 2 small limes

12 tablespoons (1 1/2 sticks) unsalted butter, cut into small pieces, at room temperature

Fresh raspberries, for garnish, optional

Confectioners' sugar, for garnish, optional

1. Preheat the oven to 375°F.

2. On a lightly floured surface, roll out the dough to a circle about ¼ inch thick and large enough just to cover the bottom and side of a 9-inch metal tart pan. Fit the dough into the pan and trim the edges. Line the bottom and sides of the shell with parchment paper. Fill the lining with dried beans, uncooked rice, or pie weights and bake in the oven for about 20 minutes. Cool and remove the weights and lining. Return the shell to the oven and bake until golden brown, 5 to 10 minutes longer.

3. Bring a saucepan of water to a boil. Meanwhile, in a large metal bowl that will fit inside the rim of the saucepan without touching the water, whisk together the whole eggs, egg yolks, 1 cup sugar, lemon and lime juices, and zests. Reduce the heat under the pan to maintain a simmer, set the bowl over but not touching the simmering water, and

continue to whisk until the mixture is very thick, about 10 minutes.

4. Turn off the heat and, still over the hot water, whisk in the butter, a few pieces at a time. (You don't want the mixture to cool down before all the butter is incorporated.) Pour the mixture through a fine-meshed sieve held over another bowl. Scrape the strained mixture from the bowl into the baked tart shell and smooth its top with a metal spatula. Let the filling cool to room temperature, then refrigerate until the filling is firm, 3 to 4 hours or as long as overnight.

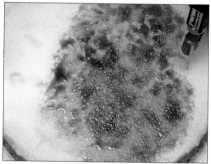

5. Just before serving, sprinkle the remaining 2 table-spoons of sugar evenly over the top of the filling. With a propane kitchen torch, or under a pre-heated broiler, caramelize the sugar until golden, watching very carefully to avoid burning the sugar. Refrigerate the tart for at least 30 min-utes to set the caramel topping. Alternatively, eliminate the 2 tablespoons of sugar and ar-range circles of raspberries on top of the tart. Sift a little confectioners' sugar over the berries just before serving.

Cookies-and-Cream Cheesecake

*I*f you love the ice cream of the same name, then you'll go crazy for this cheesecake, which combines both creamy and crunchy textures and white and dark chocolate flavors. It takes a while to make, and you really should set aside some time for it the day before you plan to serve it. But all the steps are fairly easy, and the results are really worth the effort.

CHOCOLATE CRUMBLE

1¹/₂ cups all-purpose flour

1 cup unsweetened cocoa powder

1 cup granulated sugar

¹/₄ teaspoon salt

¹/₄ pound (1 stick) unsalted butter, chilled, cut into 4 equal pieces

3 egg yolks

3 tablespoons heavy cream

CHEESECAKE

1¹/₂ pounds cream cheese, at room temperature, cut into small pieces

1 cup granulated sugar

¹/₄ teaspoon salt

³/₄ cup sour cream

3 eggs

2 teaspoons vanilla extract

4 ounces white chocolate, broken into small pieces

Fresh berries, for garnish, optional

1. Position the rack in the center of the oven and preheat the oven to 350°F. Butter or coat with nonstick spray the bottom of a 9-inch or 10-inch springform pan. Line a baking sheet with parchment paper. Set aside.

2. To make the crumble: Sift together the flour, cocoa, sugar, and salt, and transfer to the bowl of a food processor fitted with the metal blade. Process with on/off turns until blended.

Arrange the chunks of butter around the flour mixture and process until the mixture resembles coarse meal.

3. In a small cup or bowl, whisk together the egg yolks and cream. With the processor running, pour the mixture through the feed tube, making certain you scrape out all the liquid from the cup. Let the machine run until the ingredients come together to form a dough, about 1 minute. You should have about 4 cups of this crumble mixture.

4. To make the cheesecake's crust: Spoon 2 cups of the crumble mixture into the prepared pan and press evenly over the bottom. Use the bottom of a dry measuring cup to help you level the crust and give it smooth edges.

5. Spread the remaining crumble on the prepared baking sheet. Place the springform pan and baking tray in the oven and bake until the crumble is lightly toasted, 10 to 12 minutes. Turn off the oven. Transfer both the sheet and the pan to a wire rack to cool completely. When the springform pan is cool, wrap heavy-duty aluminum foil, or two layers of regular foil, around its bottom and halfway up its outside, pleating the foil to tighten it securely. Set aside. Using your hands or a fork, break up the crumble on the baking sheet into small chunks and set aside.

6. To make the filling: Put the cream cheese, sugar, and salt in the large bowl of an electric stand mixer fitted with a paddle or beaters, or in a large mixing bowl. Using the stand mixer or a handheld mixer on medium speed, beat the ingredients until smooth, stopping often to scrape down the sides of the bowl and under the blades with a rubber spatula. Turn the speed to high and continue to beat until the mixture is creamy. Stop the mixer and add the sour cream, eggs, and vanilla; beat 3 minutes longer, again stopping as necessary to scrape down the sides of the bowl and under the blades.

7. Put the pieces of white chocolate in a small microwave-proof cup or bowl. Put the container in the microwave oven, cover with a paper towel, and heat for 30 seconds. Stop and stir the chocolate. Repeat the process once or twice more, just until the chocolate is completely melted and smooth.

8. Stir the melted chocolate into the cream cheese mixture and continue to beat until well combined and smooth. You should have about 6 cups of the mixture.

9. Preheat the oven again to 350°F. Bring a kettle of water to a boil. Meanwhile, pour half the cream cheese mixture (about 3 cups) into the springform pan. Sprinkle half the chocolate crumble (about 1 cup) over the mixture. Pour in the remaining cream cheese mixture, smooth its top with a rubber spatula, and then scatter the remaining chocolate crumble evenly over its surface.

10. Place the springform pan inside a slightly larger baking pan. Using an oven glove, pull out the oven shelf and place the baking pan on it. Pour enough hot water into the baking pan to reach halfway up the sides of the springform pan, but not above the foil. Carefully slide the shelf into the oven and bake the cheesecake for 1 hour, checking the water level after about 30 minutes and topping it up if necessary. Cover the cake loosely with foil and continue to bake until its center is slightly firm, about 20 minutes longer.

11. Carefully remove the baking pan from the oven. Lift out the springform pan and place it on a wire rack to cool, carefully folding down the foil on its sides to promote quicker cooling. When the pan is cool enough to touch, completely remove the foil and continue cooling. When the cheesecake is completely cool, cover the pan loosely with a clean sheet of foil and refrigerate overnight.

12. When ready to serve, remove the cheesecake from the refrigerator. Dip a long, sharp knife in warm water and run the knife around the inside of the springform pan to loosen the cake. Remove the outer ring. Continue to dip the knife into warm water as necessary as you cut neat wedges. To serve, place a wedge of cake on a cake plate and garnish, if you like, with fresh berries.

Classic Spago Cheesecake

*I*t's not surprising that guests at the original **Spago**, the ultimate Hollywood restaurant, expected the ultimate all-American cheesecake, one that was sinfully creamy and rich. **Of course, we were happy to ex-**ceed their expectations.

BUTTER CRUNCH CRUST

1/2 cup all-purpose flour

1/4 cup finely chopped pecans or walnuts

2 tablespoons brown sugar

4 tablespoons (1/2 stick) unsalted butter, at room temperature

FILLING

11/2 pounds cream cheese, at room temperature, cut into small pieces

11/4 cups granulated sugar

1/4 teaspoon salt

3/4 cup sour cream

1 tablespoon dark rum

1 tablespoon lemon juice

2 teaspoons vanilla extract

3 eggs

Fresh berries, for garnish

1. Position the rack in the center of the oven and preheat the oven to 350°F. Butter or coat with nonstick spray the bottom of a 9-inch or 10-inch springform pan.

2. In a large bowl, assemble all the ingredients for the Butter Crunch Crust. Mix them together with your hands until the mixture resembles very small pebbles.

3. Press the Butter Crunch Crust into the bottom of the springform pan, covering the base

completely and evenly. Wrap heavy-duty aluminum foil, or two layers of regular foil, around the pan's bottom and halfway up its outside, pleating the foil to tighten it securely. Bake the crust until it is lightly golden, about 8 minutes. Remove from the oven and set aside.

4. To make the filling: Put the cream cheese, sugar, and salt in the large bowl of an electric stand mixer fitted with a paddle or beaters, or in a large mixing bowl. Using the stand mixer or a handheld mixer on medium speed, beat the ingredients until smooth, stopping often to scrape down the sides of the bowl and under the blades with a rubber spatula. Turn the speed to high and continue to  beat until the mixture is creamy. Stop the mixer and add the sour cream, rum, lemon juice, and vanilla; then, on medium speed, continue beating until well blended. Add the eggs and beat just until combined. Scrape the filling into the prepared springform pan.

5. Bring a kettle of water to a boil. Place the springform pan inside a slightly larger baking pan. Using an oven glove, pull out the oven shelf and place the baking pan on it. Pour enough hot water into the baking pan to reach halfway up the sides of the springform pan, but not above the foil. Carefully slide the shelf into the oven and bake the cheesecake until its top is lightly golden and slightly firm in the center, about 1 hour and 10 minutes. (The cake will become firmer as it cools.)

6. Carefully remove the baking pan from the oven. Lift out the springform pan and place it on a wire rack to cool, carefully folding down the foil on its sides to promote quicker cooling. When the pan is cool enough to touch, completely remove the foil and continue cooling. When the cheesecake is completely cool, cover the pan loosely with a clean sheet of foil and refrigerate overnight.

7. When ready to serve, remove the cheesecake from the refrigerator. Dip a long, sharp knife in warm water and run the knife around the inside of the springform pan to loosen the cake. Remove the outer ring. Continue to dip the knife into warm water as necessary as you cut neat wedges. To serve, place a wedge of cake on a cake plate and garnish with fresh berries of your choice. Or, for a spectacular end to a meal, cover the whole cheesecake with assorted fresh berries and present it that way at the table before slicing and serving.

Kaiserschmarren

*T*here's an interesting story behind the name of this classic Austrian soufflé-like pancake. It seems the Emperor Franz Josef liked to tear his pancakes into rough little scraps—literally, *schmarren,* which is German for trash or rubbish. So this ethereal dessert is actually called "the emperor's rubbish"! My version is more refined than some, but the presentation is still very casual. When you make it, take care to fold in the beaten egg whites just until blended, without overmixing. That guarantees the most tender results. You'll need at least one 6-inch ovenproof sauté pan to make this; four such pans will allow you to bake and serve the Kaiserschmarren all at once, a really impressive presentation.

STRAWBERRY SAUCE

1¹/₂ pounds strawberries, hulled and
   cut in halves lengthwise
¹/₄ cup dry white wine
3 tablespoons sugar
¹/₂ tablespoon grated orange zest
¹/₂ tablespoon fresh lemon juice
Juice of ¹/₂ orange
¹/₂ whole star anise

KAISERSCHMARREN

4 egg yolks
¹/₂ cup plus 1 tablespoon sugar, plus
   more for sprinkling sauté pans
¹/₄ cup crème fraîche
2 tablespoons dark rum
4 teaspoons all-purpose flour
2 tablespoons golden raisins,
   plumped in warm water for
   20 minutes, then drained
2 tablespoons unsalted butter,
   melted, for brushing sauté pans
3 egg whites

1. Up to a day or two ahead, make the Strawberry Sauce: In a medium saucepan, combine ½ pound of the strawberries with the wine, sugar, orange zest, lemon and orange juices, and star anise. Bring to a boil over medium-high heat and cook, stirring frequently, for 5 minutes. Remove from the heat, cover, and let the mixture steep for 10 minutes. Transfer the mixture to a blender or food processor and process until thoroughly blended. Pour the sauce through a fine-meshed strainer set over a nonreactive bowl. Cover with plastic wrap and refrigerate until ready to use.

2. Up to 1 day ahead, make the Kaiserschmarren base: In a mixing bowl, combine the egg yolks and 6 tablespoons of sugar. With a stand or hand-held electric mixer on medium speed, beat until the yolks are pale yellow. Add the crème fraîche and rum and continue to mix until smooth. Fold in the flour and raisins. Cover with plastic wrap and refrigerate until ready to use.

3. Preheat the oven to 425°F. Brush one to four 6-inch ovenproof sauté pans or gratin dishes with 2 tablespoons butter and sprinkle them generously and evenly with sugar.

4. To make the Kaiserschmarren, in a separate clean mixing bowl, whisk or beat the egg whites until they form soft, drooping peaks when the whisk or beaters are lifted out. Add the remaining 3 tablespoons of sugar and continue to whip until the egg whites form stiff but not dry peaks. Using a rubber spatula, gently fold this meringue into the base just until it is barely incorporated, cutting the spatula blade down into the center of the bowl, along the bottom, and up the side, turning the bowl after each fold. Spoon one fourth of the mixture into each sauté pan. Bake until the Kaiserschmarren are puffed and golden, about 12 minutes. Repeat if necessary until all the batter is used.

5. While the Kaiserschmarren are baking, reheat the Strawberry Sauce in a medium saucepan over medium heat. Add the remaining pound of fresh strawberries and toss or stir briefly to coat them with the sauce. When the Kaiserschmarren are done, spoon the sauce onto each serving plate. With a spatula or large spoon, scoop the Kaiserschmarren in large chunks from the pans onto each plate.

Salzburger Nockerln with Fresh Raspberry Jam

*S*alzburg is a wonderful town on the Bavarian border famous for its small hills, known in Austrian as *nockerln*. This traditional Austrian dessert celebrates those hills with its gently rolling heaps of meringue that taste indulgently rich and utterly delicious. Whenever I eat it, I'm filled with happy memories of good times with loved ones. I hope the dessert inspires some wonderful memories for you, too.

FRESH RASPBERRY JAM

12 ounces fresh raspberries
   (about 2 baskets)

1/4 cup sugar

1/4 cup fresh orange juice

2 tablespoons fresh lemon juice

SALZBURGER NOCKERLN

3/4 cup plus 2 tablespoons sugar

2 tablespoons tapioca flour, sifted

4 egg yolks

2 tablespoons Grand Marnier or other
   orange-flavored liqueur

1 tablespoon grated orange zest

1 tablespoon grated lemon zest

8 egg whites

Confectioners' sugar, for garnish

Whipped cream, for garnish

Fresh berries, for garnish

1. To make the Fresh Raspberry Jam: In a small sauté pan, combine half of the raspberries with the sugar, orange juice, and lemon juice. Bring to a boil over medium-high heat and cook for about 3 minutes, whisking vigorously to break up the raspberries. The mixture should resemble a loose jam. Remove from the heat and gently stir in the remaining raspberries until well coated. Set aside.

2. Preheat the oven to 400°F.

3. To make the Nockerln: Pour about two thirds of the warm raspberry jam into a 7 by 11-inch baking dish. In a medium mixing bowl, whisk together 2 tablespoons of sugar and the tapioca flour. Add the egg yolks, Grand Marnier, and orange and lemon zests. Whisk until the mixture is well blended and light yellow in color.

4. In an electric mixer fitted with a wire whisk, or in a clean mixing bowl with an electric hand mixer, beat together the egg whites and 2 tablespoons of sugar at medium speed until they form soft peaks that droop when the beater is lifted out. While continuing to beat the whites, add the remaining sugar in a slow, steady stream. Keep beating until the whites form stiff peaks.

5. Stir a third of the beaten egg whites into the egg yolk mixture to blend. Then, gently fold in the remaining whites until well blended.

6. Spoon the egg mixture in hill-shaped mounds on top of the raspberry jam in the baking dish. Bake until the nockerln are well risen and golden, 12 to 15 minutes.

7. As soon as the nockerln are done, dust them with some confectioners' sugar by spooning the sugar into a small, fine-meshed sieve held over the baking dish, then tapping the sieve. Present the nockerln in their baking dish at the table, spooning them onto serving plates and garnishing each serving with some of the remaining raspberry jam, whipped cream, and a few fresh berries.

White Chocolate Malt Ice Cream

*O*ne taste of this ice cream will remind you of a classic malted milkshake. You can also add a teaspoon of vanilla extract to the mixture, stirring it in just before freezing it. Or substitute milk or dark chocolate for the white chocolate. Your favorite chocolate or hot fudge sauce can only make it even better, so go wild!

2 cups whole milk

2 cups heavy cream

8 egg yolks

10 ounces white chocolate, broken or cut into small chunks

1/2 cup malt powder

1. In a large, heavy saucepan over medium-high heat, bring the milk and cream to a boil. Remove from the heat.

2. In a large stainless-steel mixing bowl, whisk the egg yolks until smooth. While continuing to whisk, slowly pour in the hot milk-cream mixture. Return the mixture to the saucepan and cook over medium heat, stirring occasionally, until it is thick enough to coat the back of a wooden spoon.

3. Put the chocolate in a microwave-proof bowl. Cover the bowl with a paper towel, put it in the microwave, and cook for 30 seconds; stir the mixture. Repeat one to three times more, just until the chocolate is smoothly melted. Whisk the melted chocolate into the hot ice-cream mixture. Pour 1 cup of the liquid into a heatproof measuring cup, add the malt to the cup, and stir until it is completely dissolved. Return the malted mixture to the saucepan and stir well. Pour the mixture through a fine-meshed strainer into a large heatproof mixing bowl. Set the bowl inside a larger bowl containing ice and water and chill it, stirring occasionally, until the mixture is completely cold.

4. Transfer the mixture to an ice-cream machine and freeze it, following the manufacturer's directions.

Almond Granita

*T*he beautiful thing about a granita is that you don't even have to own a home ice-cream machine to make a great frozen dessert. You just freeze it in a metal pan, stirring and scraping it up occasionally to form the refreshing granular crystals that give the dessert its name. This almond-flavored version, which I discovered on a visit to Sicily for my TV show on the Food Network, provides a wonderful, light-yet-rich, and surprisingly soothing finish to a meal in which strong or spicy seasonings are featured. If you can't find almond meal, substitute another 1/2 pound whole blanched almonds, put them with the 1/4 cup sugar in a food processor fitted with the metal blade, and pulse just until finely ground.

ALMOND MILK

1 quart whole milk

1/2 pound almond meal

1/2 pound whole blanched almonds

2 tablespoons almond extract

1/4 cup sugar

2 ounces almond paste

1/4 cup sugar

2 teaspoons fresh lemon juice

1. First, make the Almond Milk: In a saucepan over medium-low heat, bring the milk to a slow boil. Stir in the almond meal and whole almonds; reduce the heat and simmer gently for 30 minutes. Turn off the heat, cover the pan, and leave the mixture to steep for 20 minutes. Using an immersion blender, process the mixture until pureed; alternatively, transfer it to a blender, in batches if necessary, and process, taking care to avoid splattering. Line a fine-meshed sieve with dampened cheesecloth, place it over a mixing bowl, and pour the mixture through it, pressing down on the solids to extract all the liquid. Stir in the almond extract and sugar. Place the bowl inside a larger bowl filled with ice and water and chill, stirring occasionally, until the almond milk is completely cold.

2. Put the cold almond milk in a blender and add the almond paste, sugar, and lemon juice. Process until smooth.

3. Transfer the granita mixture to one or two metal baking pans large enough so that the liquid is no more than ¼ to ½ inch deep. Put it in the freezer. Every 20 to 30 minutes, stir the

mixture with a spoon, scraping up the crystals that have formed on the bottom and sides of the pan.

4. When the granita is completely frozen, scoop it into individual chilled serving bowls or dessert glasses. To store it, transfer to an airtight freezer container. You may have to re-scrape the stored granita with a fork or spoon to refresh its granular consistency before serving.

Melon Granita

*Y*ou won't believe how fresh this frozen dessert tastes. It's like a just-picked melon, magically transformed into scoops of glistening crystals that you can make right in your freezer, without the use of an ice-cream machine. Serve it as a light end to a meal. Or for a very special occasion, offer small scoops betweens savory courses to cleanse the palate. For the melon juice, puree fresh fruit in a blender or processor, then strain it. Some health-food markets also sell bottles of fresh-squeezed melon juice.

4½ cups honeydew melon juice or
    watermelon juice
¼ cup sugar

1 to 2 tablespoons lemon juice
¼ cup Midori melon liqueur

1. Put the melon juice in a mixing bowl. Stir in sugar and lemon juice to taste, keeping in mind that freezing will mute the flavor slightly. Stir in the liqueur.

2. Transfer the granita mixture to one or two metal baking pans large enough so that the liquid is no more than ¼ to ½ inch deep. Put it in the freezer. Every 20 to 30 minutes, stir the mixture with a spoon, scraping up the crystals that have formed on the bottom and sides of the pan.

3. When the granita is completely frozen, scoop it into individual chilled serving bowls or dessert glasses. To store it, transfer to an airtight freezer container. You may have to re-scrape the stored granita with a fork or spoon to refresh its granular consistency before serving.

Chicken Stock

Brown Chicken Stock

Fish Stock

Brown Veal Stock

Court Bouillon

Basic Pasta Dough

Pizza Dough

Puff Pastry

Sugar Dough

Peeled and Seeded Tomatoes and Tomato Concassé

Oven-Dried Tomatoes

Roasted Whole Garlic

Double-Blanched Garlic

Toasting Nuts

Toasting and Grinding Whole Spices

Making a Bouquet Garni

Basil Oil

Chili and Garlic Oil

Dill Cream

Basil-Garlic Vinaigrette

Greek Salad Dressing

Cutting Julienne and Chiffonade

Pitting an Avocado

Pitting Olives

Preparing Artichoke Hearts

Shelling and Deveining Shrimp

Chicken Stock

*C*hicken stock is one of the most important and versatile ingredients any cook can have, a wonderful source of flavor and moisture and the foundation for all kinds of soups and sauces. Although it seems like a lot of work to prepare such a basic ingredient, the difference between homemade and store-bought stocks can be huge. Stock can be stored refrigerated in a covered container for up to 3 days. Or it can be frozen in resealable plastic storage bags, making sure to eliminate any headspace of air from the bags before sealing.

5 to 6 pounds chicken bones, including necks and feet, coarsely chopped

About 3 1/2 quarts cold water

1 medium carrot, peeled and sliced

1 medium onion, peeled and quartered

1 small celery stalk, sliced

1 small leek, thoroughly washed and sliced

3 sprigs of parsley, with stems

1 bay leaf

1/2 teaspoon whole white peppercorns

1. Put the chicken bones in a 6-quart stockpot and pour in the water to cover. Put the pot over medium-high heat and bring it to a rolling boil, regularly skimming off the scum that rises to the surface as the liquid heats.

2. Add the remaining ingredients, reduce the heat, and simmer for about 2 hours, skimming as necessary.

3. Strain the stock through a fine-meshed strainer into a clean pot or large heatproof bowl. Let it come to room temperature, then cover and refrigerate overnight. Discard the hardened layer of fat that forms on the surface. Strain the stock into a clean bowl and use as needed.

Brown Chicken Stock

MAKES ABOUT 2 CUPS

*T*o make **Brown Chicken Stock**, follow the recipe for **Chicken Stock (page 204)**. However, before putting the ingredients in the pot, spread the chicken bones and onion pieces in a roasting pan and roast them in an oven preheated to 400°F, turning occasionally, until the bones are a deep golden brown, about 30 minutes, taking care not to let them burn. After transferring the ingredients to the stockpot, place the roasting pan on the stove over medium heat, add 2 cups of the water, and stir and scrape to deglaze the pan deposits; add the liquid to the pot. After simmering the stock for 3 hours, straining, and cooling it, pour it into an ice-cube tray and freeze. Transfer the cubes to an airtight, heavy-duty plastic bag and return to the freezer. Remove cubes as needed and defrost them before use.

Fish Stock

*F*or the best flavor, use the skeletons of saltwater fish such as sole, John Dory, turbot, halibut, or other very fresh, nonoily fish. A good fish market will reserve the bones from filleted fish and will sell them to you for a very small price, or even give them to you with another purchase. Fish Stock will keep in the refrigerator for 2 to 3 days or frozen for 2 to 3 weeks. After that time, its flavor begins to fade.

2 pounds fish skeletons, cut into
   pieces
2 tablespoons vegetable oil
1 small carrot, peeled and sliced
1/2 medium onion, peeled and sliced

1 small stalk celery, sliced
2 cups dry white wine
About 1 quart cold water
1 bouquet garni (page 223)

1. Clean the fish bones under cold running water, removing the gills from the head and any traces of blood from the frames.

2. In a large saucepan, heat the oil over low heat. Add the fish bones and vegetables, cover the pan, and sweat them for 10 minutes, stirring them once or twice to prevent browning.

3. Add the wine to the pan and stir and scrape to deglaze any deposits. Add enough water to cover the bones and vegetables by 2 inches. Add the bouquet garni and bring the liquid to a boil, skimming away the scum as it rises to the surface. Reduce the heat and simmer the stock for 20 to 25 minutes.

4. Strain the stock through a fine-meshed strainer into a clean saucepan. Bring it to a boil and reduce it over medium heat to 1 quart.

Brown Veal Stock

*V*eal stock has a full but neutral flavor and may be used in place of beef stock, in lamb or duck dishes, or even as a richer-tasting replacement for chicken stock. Ask the butcher to cut up the bones for you. Refrigerate the stock for 2 to 3 days or freeze it in small quantities for 2 to 3 months.

10 pounds veal bones, cut into 2-inch pieces

2 onions, peeled and quartered

2 carrots, coarsely chopped

1 stalk celery, coarsely chopped

1 leek, thoroughly cleaned and coarsely chopped

2 tomatoes, quartered

2 bay leaves

1 teaspoon whole black peppercorns

2 sprigs of thyme

1 head garlic, halved, optional

1 gallon water

1. Preheat the oven to 450°F.

2. In a large roasting pan, spread the bones and onions in an even layer. Put the pan in the oven and roast the bones until dark golden brown all over, turning them several times as they brown, about 1½ hours. Transfer the bones to a large stockpot and add the carrots, celery, leek, tomatoes, bay leaves, peppercorns, thyme, and, if desired, the garlic.

3. Pour off the fat from the roasting pan. Add 2 cups of the water and, over medium-high heat, stir and scrape with a wooden spoon to deglaze the pan deposits. Add this liquid to the stockpot and pour in enough water to cover the bones by 2 inches. Bring the water to a boil, reduce the heat, and let the mixture simmer very gently for at least 6 hours and as long as 24 hours, skimming away foam and fat from the surface as necessary and adding enough extra water to keep the bones covered.

4. Strain the liquid through a fine-meshed sieve into a clean stockpot. Skim off any last traces of foam or fat. Bring the stock to a boil, then turn down the heat to low and reduce the stock until it has a full-bodied flavor. You should have about 2 quarts.

Court Bouillon

*U*se this quickly prepared, fragrant liquid to poach or steam fish or other foods in a health-conscious way with no added fat.

2 medium carrots

2 stalks celery

1 leek, thoroughly washed

1 sprig of fresh thyme or pinch of
    dried thyme

1 bay leaf

1 teaspoon salt

1/2 teaspoon freshly ground black
    pepper

2 quarts water

2 cups dry white wine

1. Slice the carrots, celery, and leek into ¼-inch pieces. Put them in a saucepan.

2. Add the remaining ingredients and bring to a boil. Continue boiling for 20 minutes, until the liquid is flavorful.

Basic Pasta Dough

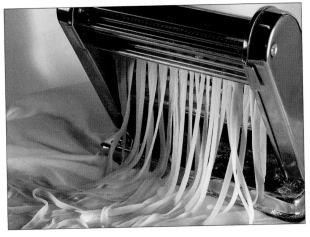

*M*aking pasta can be fun, and it is easy to involve the whole family in the preparation. If you'd like a firmer dough, make it with half all-purpose flour and half fine semolina, a flour ground from hard durum wheat. (To make green pasta, replace the water with fresh spinach juice, which you can buy in health food stores or make by pureeing ¹/₂ pound of clean, raw fresh spinach in a food processor and then squeezing it inside a linen towel or napkin. Reserve the napkin for this purpose, as the spinach will stain it.) Use this very basic recipe for fettuccine, lasagne, ravioli, or any other shape you choose. For the best results, always follow the instructions that come with your pasta machine.

3 cups all-purpose flour

8 large egg yolks

1 teaspoon kosher salt

1 teaspoon extra-virgin olive oil

About ¹/₄ cup water

Semolina or all-purpose flour, for dusting

1. In a food processor fitted with the metal blade, combine the flour, egg yolks, salt, olive oil, and 3 tablespoons of the water. Process until the dough begins to hold together, then stop the machine and pinch the dough to test it. If it feels too dry, add up to 1 more tablespoon of water and process until it forms a moist ball. Turn out the dough onto a lightly floured smooth work surface and knead by hand until the dough forms a smooth ball. Loosely wrap the ball in plastic wrap and let it rest at room temperature for 20 minutes to 1 hour.

2. Cut the dough into 4 equal pieces. Keep the other pieces covered in plastic while you roll

out one piece at a time, by hand with a rolling pin or through the rollers of a pasta machine, stretching the dough to the desired thickness.

3. If using a pasta machine, set the rollers at the widest opening. Flatten the first piece of dough into a thick strip no wider than the machine, to enable it to pass through the rollers. If necessary, dust the pasta very lightly with flour. Run the pasta through the machine. Fold in thirds, crosswise, and run through the machine again. Repeat this procedure two more times, until the dough is smooth and somewhat elastic. Set the rollers to the next smaller opening and run the dough through the rollers. Continue rolling and stretching the dough, using a smaller opening each time and dusting lightly with flour only as necessary, until the next to the last or the last setting is reached. (The strip of dough will be long. If you don't have enough space on your worktable, halfway through the rolling process cut the strip of dough in half and continue to work with each piece separately, keeping the unused dough covered.)

4. Adjust the cutting mechanism to the desired width of pasta, cut the noodles, and allow them to dry before cooking. A convenient way to dry pasta is to arrange the cut pasta on a pastry tray sprinkled with flour, preferably semolina. As one layer is completed, sprinkle flour over the noodles, place a piece of parchment paper over them, and continue layering with noodles and flour. Air-dry for at least 15 to 20 minutes.

5. Repeat with the remaining pieces of dough.

Pizza Dough

...$\mathcal{W}$ith this recipe, you can make four individual pizzas, as described below, or divide the dough in half and make two large 12-inch pizzas. The baking time will be the same. The dough-mixing instructions allow you to use either a stand mixer or a food processor. Chopped fresh basil, chopped sun-dried tomatoes, or a sprinkling of crushed red pepper flakes can be added to the dough with the flour, if desired, for additional flavor. Be creative with your pizzas!

1 package active dry or fresh yeast

1 teaspoon honey

1 cup warm water (105°F to 115°F)

3 cups all-purpose flour

1 teaspoon kosher salt

1 tablespoon extra-virgin olive oil, plus more for brushing

Toppings of your choice (see pizza recipes, pages 52 to 55)

1. In a small bowl, dissolve the yeast and honey in ¼ cup of the warm water.

2. In a mixer fitted with a dough hook, combine the flour and the salt. Add the oil, yeast mixture, and the remaining ¾ cup of water and mix on low speed until the dough comes cleanly away from the sides of the bowl and clusters around the dough hook, about 5 minutes. (The pizza dough can also be made in a food processor. Dissolve the yeast as above. Combine the flour and salt in the bowl of a food processor fitted with the metal blade. Pulse once or twice, add the remaining ingredients, and process until the dough begins to form a ball that rides around the side of the bowl on top of the blade.)

3. Turn the dough out onto a clean work surface and knead by hand 2 or 3 minutes longer. The dough should feel smooth and firm. Cover the dough with a clean, damp towel and let it rise in a warm spot for about 30 minutes. (When ready, the dough should stretch easily as it is lightly pulled.)

4. Place a pizza stone on the middle rack of the oven and preheat the oven to 500°F.

5. Divide the dough into 4 balls, about 6 ounces each. Work each ball by pulling down the sides and tucking them under the bottom of the ball. Repeat four or five times to form a smooth, even, firm ball. Then, on a smooth, unfloured surface, roll the ball under the palm of your hand until the top of the dough is smooth and firm, about 1 minute. Cover the

dough with a damp towel and let it rest for 15 to 20 minutes. At this point, the balls can be wrapped in plastic and refrigerated for up to 2 days.

6. To prepare a pizza, dip the ball of dough into flour, shake off the excess flour, place the dough on a clean, lightly floured surface, and start to stretch the dough. Press down on the center, spreading the dough into an 8-inch circle, with its outer rim a little thicker than the inner circle. If you find this difficult to do, use a small rolling pin to roll out the dough. Lightly brush the inner circle of the dough with oil and arrange the toppings of your choice over the inner circle.

7. Using a lightly floured baker's peel or a rimless flat baking tray, slide the pizza onto the baking stone and bake until the pizza crust is nicely browned, 10 to 12 minutes. Remember that the oven is very hot and be careful as you move the pizza into and out of the oven. Transfer the pizza to a firm surface and cut into slices with a pizza cutter or very sharp knife. Serve immediately.

Puff Pastry

.. *I* recommend preparing a large amount of this extremely versatile pastry at one time and cutting it into desired quantities and shapes for freezing. (It freezes very successfully. Remove it from the freezer and place in the refrigerator the day before you plan to use it.) Cut into squares called feuilletées, it can also be used to make many different desserts—with various fruits, ice creams, and sweet sauces.

PASTRY BASE

1³/₄ cups pastry flour

1³/₄ cups all-purpose flour

1/2 teaspoon salt

²/₃ pound (1¹/₃ sticks) chilled unsalted butter, cut into small pieces

1 to 1¹/₄ cups ice water

BUTTER BLOCK

7/8 pound (3¹/₂ sticks) unsalted butter, chilled (it helps to keep the butter in sticks for making the block)

1. To make the pastry base: In a food processor fitted with the metal blade, combine the pastry flour, all-purpose flour, and salt. Add the butter pieces and pulse the machine a few times until the mixture resembles coarse meal.

2. With the machine running, pour just enough iced water through the feed tube to make a stiff but pliable dough. (This amount of water can vary quite a lot, so start out with 1 cup and add up to the extra ¼ cup.) Turn the dough out onto a very lightly floured board. Shape it into a flattened ball and wrap tightly in plastic wrap. Refrigerate overnight.

3. To prepare the butter block: Arrange the sticks of butter into as much of a square as possible. Wrap

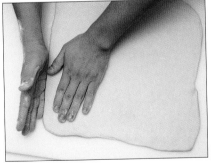

in a clean cotton kitchen towel or napkin to absorb excess moisture. With a heavy rolling pin, pound the butter to form an 8-inch square about 1 inch thick. With the help of the rolling pin, even out the sides as necessary. Wrap in plastic wrap and chill in the refrigerator.

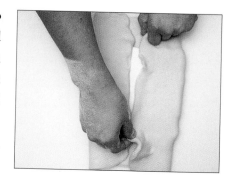

4. Remove the pastry base and the butter block from the refrigerator and bring them to room temperature before using. Both should be at the same temperature and consistency before rolling.

5. Lightly flour the pastry board and rolling pin. Roll out the pastry base to an 18-inch square. Remove the butter from the towel and place it in the middle of the pastry base. Fold two opposite sides over to meet in the center of the butter. If the overlapping ends are too thick, level them off by lightly moving the rolling pin over the ends. Even the two remaining opposite ends and fold them to meet in the center, stretching as necessary until the seams come together. The butter block will be completely and neatly enclosed in the pastry.

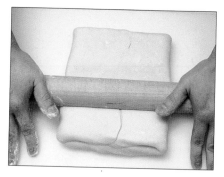

6. Roll out the pastry to a rectangle about 18 by 12 inches. Starting at a 12-inch side, fold the dough into thirds. Turn the dough so that the seam is on your right and again roll out to the same-size rectangle, sprinkling the pastry board and dough very lightly with flour as necessary to prevent the dough from sticking. Using a large, dry pastry brush, brush away excess flour before and after folding. Using the rolling pin, even out the pastry as it is being rolled. Press two indentations in the dough with a knuckle or fingertip, to remind you that you have made two turns of the dough, and

wrap the dough securely in plastic wrap. Refrigerate for at least 4 hours or overnight.

7. Remove the pastry from the refrigerator and let it soften slightly at room temperature. With the seam on your right, again complete two more turns. Press four indentations into the dough, rewrap it in plastic wrap, and refrigerate for at least 2 hours. Again, let the dough soften slightly and roll one more time to complete a fifth turn. At this point, the pastry can be cut, wrapped, and frozen for future use. When ready to use the pastry, remove from the freezer and refrigerate overnight. Use as needed.

Sugar Dough

■ ■ *Like a delicious butter cookie, this dough is ideal for a wide variety of piecrusts and other pastries.*

2¹/₃ cups cake flour or pastry flour

¹/₃ cup sugar

¹/₂ pound (2 sticks) unsalted butter, chilled, cut into small pieces

2 egg yolks

1 to 2 tablespoons heavy cream

1. In a food processor fitted with the metal blade, combine the flour and sugar. Add the butter and pulse the machine until the mixture resembles fine meal.

2. In a small bowl, whisk together the yolks and 1 tablespoon of the cream. Scrape into the machine and process until a ball of dough begins to form; if necessary, use some or all of the additional cream to help the dough come together. Remove the dough from the machine and, on a lightly floured surface, pat and press it down into a flat, circular disk. Wrap in plastic wrap and refrigerate for at least 1 hour. Use as needed.

Peeled and Seeded Tomatoes and Tomato Concassé

*T*he French verb *concasser* means literally to chop coarsely or to pound. In the kitchen, "concassé" most often refers to tomatoes that have been chopped after peeling and seeding them. Doing this will concentrate the flavor of even raw tomatoes. And when **Tomato Concassé** is added to a cooked dish, the tomatoes break down, cook, and spread through the dish more evenly.

1. Bring a pot of water to a boil. Fill a large mixing bowl with ice and water. With a small, sharp knife, score a shallow *X* in the flower end of each tomato.

2. Add the tomatoes to the boiling water and blanch them for about 30 seconds. Drain the tomatoes and immediately plunge them into the bowl of ice water.

3. Drain the tomatoes and, starting at the scored *X*, peel them, using your fingertips or, if necessary, the knife. Cut out the cores. Cut the tomatoes lengthwise into quarters and, with your fingertip, remove their seeds.

4. Cut the quartered tomatoes lengthwise into uniform slices ½ to ¼ inch wide. Cut across the slices in the same uniform width to make even dice.

Oven-Dried Tomatoes

I find that unlike sun-dried tomatoes, these oven-dried gems have a much sweeter and more natural tomato flavor. Use them to enhance pasta, pizzas, seafood, meats, or poultry. For the best and tastiest results, make them when summer's sun-ripened tomatoes are at their peak; the recipe can be doubled or tripled if you desire. The tomatoes will keep 2 to 3 days, refrigerated, in a covered container.

12 medium Roma tomatoes
(about 2 pounds)

3/4 cup extra-virgin olive oil, plus
more as needed

1 teaspoon minced fresh thyme leaves

6 garlic cloves, crushed and peeled

1/2 teaspoon kosher salt

1/4 teaspoon freshly ground black
pepper

1/2 teaspoon sugar

1. Preheat the oven to 250°F. Meanwhile, bring a pot of water to a boil. Fill a large mixing bowl with ice and water. With a small, sharp knife, score a shallow *X* in the flower end of each tomato.

2. Add the tomatoes to the boiling water and blanch them for about 30 seconds. Drain the tomatoes and immediately plunge them into the bowl of ice water.

3. Drain the tomatoes and, starting at the scored *X,* peel them, using your fingertips or, if necessary, the knife. Cut out the cores. Cut the tomatoes lengthwise into quarters and, with your fingertip, remove their seeds.

4. Line a baking sheet with parchment paper and arrange the tomato quarters on the tray, cut side down. Drizzle the tomatoes with ¼ cup of the olive oil and sprinkle them with thyme and garlic. In a small bowl, stir together the salt, pepper, and sugar and sprinkle the mixture evenly over the tomatoes.

5. Bake the tomatoes until they begin to shrivel and have darkened to a deep red color, about 1 hour. Remove them from the oven and, when they are cool enough to handle, transfer them to a nonreactive container. Pour the remaining ½ cup of olive oil over the tomatoes to cover them completely, and then cover the container. Refrigerate and use as needed.

Roasted Whole Garlic

*R*oasting garlic develops a sweet, mellow, full flavor without raw garlic's familiar harshness. Store it in the refrigerator, covered, for up to 3 days.

4 whole heads garlic   **About ¹/₃ cup extra-virgin olive oil**

1. Preheat the oven to 375°F.
2. Arrange the garlic heads in a small roasting pan and toss them with the olive oil, coating them well.
3. Roast the garlic until very tender, 50 to 60 minutes. Remove from the oven and leave them to cool at room temperature. When the garlic is cool enough to handle, use a serrated knife to cut the heads in half, crosswise. Remove the softened garlic pulp from the skins, either by squeezing each half or by scooping the garlic out with a tiny spoon or small knife.

4. Transfer the puree-soft roasted garlic to a container, cover, and refrigerate. Use as needed.

Double-Blanched Garlic

*H*ow do you enjoy all of garlic's wonderful flavor without the shock of its pungent bite? Here's one easy but effective way, which results in cloves that are tender but still crunchy.

Whole garlic cloves   **Kosher salt**

1. Prepare a bowl of ice water.
2. With a small, sharp knife, trim off the ends of as many garlic cloves as you need. Without putting the garlic in yet, pour enough cold water into a small saucepan to cover the cloves completely. Salt the water lightly and bring it to a boil over medium-high heat. Carefully drop in the garlic cloves and blanch them for 30 seconds.

3. With a slotted spoon, remove the garlic cloves from the boiling water and immediately plunge them into the ice water to stop the cooking process.
4. Repeat the boiling process and once again cool the garlic by plunging it into the ice water. Drain the garlic and dry it well. The peels should slip off easily. Cut the garlic into slices and use as needed.

Toasting Nuts

$\mathcal{T}$■ ■ oasting nuts gives them a richer flavor, more attractive golden color, and crunchier texture.

1. Put the nuts in a small, heavy, ungreased skillet just large enough to hold them in a single layer. Place the skillet over low heat.

2. Cook the nuts, stirring almost continuously to prevent burning. Remove the nuts from the heat and transfer them to a bowl to cool when they are a shade or two lighter than the final desired shade, as their residual heat will continue to toast them. Total toasting time may range from 2 to 5 minutes, depending on the size of the nuts.

Toasting and Grinding Whole Spices

*..W*hile small containers of already-ground spices will work well for many recipes, some recipes call for whole spices, which are then toasted to develop a fuller flavor and ground to release that flavor just before cooking.

1. Put the spices in a small, heavy, ungreased skillet just large enough to hold them in a single layer. Put the skillet over medium-low heat.
2. Toast the spices, stirring constantly, until they are fragrant, no more than a minute or two. Transfer them to a bowl and continue stirring to cool them down.
3. When the spices are cool, grind them to a powder in an electric spice mill or by pounding them in a mortar with a pestle.

Making a Bouquet Garni

*M*any recipes for stocks, soups, stews, and braises call for a bouquet garni, a bundle of aromatic herbs that flavor the liquid as it cooks and can be easily plucked out before serving. How you assemble one will depend on the size of the bouquet garni and its ingredients.

1. For a bouquet garni that includes smaller ingredients that might get lost in the cooking liquid, tie them together inside a square of cheesecloth. First, cut a square of cheesecloth about 8 by 8 inches. Put the ingredients in the center of the square, gather the corners and sides neatly together, and tie them securely with a piece of kitchen string.

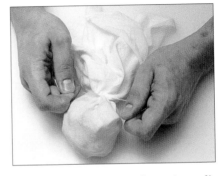

2. For a good-sized bouquet garni that features fresh herbs and other leafy or large ingredients with stems or stalks, gather the ingredients together just like a bouquet. With kitchen string, tie the stems or stalks securely together, looping the string tightly around them several times before making a knot.

Basil Oil

MAKES ABOUT 1½ CUPS

*B*right green and fragrant, this oil adds a wonderful look and flavor when drizzled onto seafood dishes such as Acqua Pazza (page 94) and vegetable soups. It will keep in an airtight container in your refrigerator for 2 to 3 weeks.

2 cups basil leaves, packed

1 cup extra-virgin olive oil

1. Bring a saucepan of water to a boil. Prepare a bowl filled with ice and water.

2. Blanch the basil leaves in the boiling water for just 2 seconds. Drain them and immediately refresh the basil leaves in the bowl of ice water. Drain well. Line a baking sheet with paper towels and arrange the basil leaves on the tray in a single layer to dry for 1 hour.

3. Pour the oil into a blender. Turn on the machine, at the "puree" setting if it has one, and gradually add the blanched basil leaves. Continue to process until the leaves are evenly pureed and well blended with the oil. Transfer the mixture to a squeeze bottle and let it steep for a few hours before using as needed.

Chili and Garlic Oil

.. *B*rush this flavorful oil on pizza dough or blend it into pasta dough. It can also be used for sautéing ingredients to toss with pasta. The oil will keep in a covered container in the refrigerator for 2 to 3 weeks.

1 whole head garlic (about
2¹/2 ounces), cloves separated
and peeled

2 cups extra-virgin olive oil
1 tablespoon red pepper flakes

1. In a small saucepan, combine the garlic cloves and olive oil. Bring to a boil over high heat, then reduce the heat to maintain a bare simmer and cook until the garlic turns golden brown, 10 to 15 minutes. Keep a close watch: if the garlic gets too dark, the oil will have a bitter taste.

2. Let the oil cool, then stir in the red pepper flakes. Leave at room temperature for at least 2 hours to let the flavors blend. Strain the oil into a clean glass container, cover, and refrigerate.

Dill Cream

*S*spread just a couple of tablespoons of this tasty cream over cooked pizza dough before topping it with smoked salmon to make my signature Pizza with Smoked Salmon and Caviar (page 54). You'll probably make more than one of those pizzas for a special meal, and this recipe will still give you plenty. You're bound to find other uses. Try spreading it on potato pancakes or savory crepes, for example. The cream will keep well in the refrigerator for up to 1 week.

1½ cups sour cream

3 tablespoons minced shallots

2 tablespoons chopped fresh dill
 leaves

1½ tablespoons fresh lemon juice

¼ teaspoon freshly ground white
 pepper

1. In a medium bowl, combine all the ingredients and mix well.
2. Cover with plastic wrap and refrigerate until ready to use.

Basil-Garlic Vinaigrette

*T*ry this simple dressing over sliced sun-ripened tomatoes, a tomato-and-mozzarella salad, or your own favorite combination of salad vegetables. It also makes a wonderful marinade for chicken or shrimp, as you can see in my recipe for Grilled Italian Chicken (page 110).

1/2 cup chopped fresh basil leaves

1/4 cup champagne vinegar

2 tablespoons chopped garlic

2 tablespoons freshly grated
    Parmesan cheese

1/2 cup extra-virgin olive oil

Salt

Freshly ground pepper

1. In a blender or the bowl of a food processor fitted with the metal blade, combine the basil, vinegar, garlic, and Parmesan cheese. Process until the basil is finely pureed, stopping to scrape down the bowl as necessary.

2. With the motor running, slowly pour in the olive oil. Continue processing until smooth. Season to taste with salt and pepper. If not using immediately, briefly whisk the ingredients to blend them together again before use.

Greek Salad Dressing

MAKES ABOUT 3½ CUPS

*P*lease don't restrict this dressing for my **Greek Shrimp Salad (page 40)** to that recipe alone; any you have left over will keep for several days in an airtight container in the refrigerator. You'll find it just as wonderful with a simple mixed green salad, or as a marinade for grilled poultry or seafood. When marinating with it, however, don't leave foods in for more than a couple of hours, as the acidity of the yogurt will begin to make them too soft.

1 cup plain yogurt

1/3 cup fresh lemon juice

1/4 cup **Dijon** mustard

1/4 cup red wine vinegar

2 tablespoons minced garlic

1 tablespoon minced fresh dill leaves

1 tablespoon minced fresh parsley leaves

1 tablespoon minced fresh thyme leaves

1/2 teaspoon kosher salt

1/4 teaspoon freshly ground white pepper

1 1/2 cups extra-virgin olive oil

Sugar

1. In a medium nonreactive bowl, whisk together the yogurt, lemon juice, mustard, vinegar, garlic, dill, parsley, thyme, salt, and pepper.

2. Whisking continuously, slowly pour in the oil. Stir in a little sugar to taste, to highlight the lemon flavor. Cover with plastic wrap and refrigerate until ready to use. Briefly whisk again to reblend the ingredients before use.

228 ▪ LIVE, LOVE, EAT!

Cutting Julienne and Chiffonade

Many recipes call for vegetables to be cut into strips known in the professional kitchen by the French words "julienne" and "chiffonade." The difference between the two terms lies not only in the width of the strips but also in the type of vegetables.

Julienne strips are sometimes referred to by the English as "matchsticks," which gives a pretty clear idea of their size: $1/8$ inch wide and thick, and 1 to 2 inches long for regular julienne, and $1/16$ inch wide and thick for fine julienne.

Although julienne can refer to thin strips of leaves, such as fresh basil, most leaves cut into strips are usually called a chiffonade—literally, "ruffles."

To cut any julienne and chiffonade, use a good, sharp chef's knife with a slightly curved blade that allows you to rock it slightly while cutting.

1. To cut a vegetable into julienne strips, first cut it into uniformly thin slices. Then stack the slices and cut across them at the same uniform thinness to make julienne strips of identical thickness and width. Or stack or roll up leaves such as basil and cut across them to make strips of the desired width.

2. To cut a chiffonade of leaves, stack several leaves neatly together and then roll them up into a compact bundle. Cut the bundle crosswise in identical thinness to get strips that unfurl into a uniform chiffonade.

Pitting an Avocado

*H*ow many times have you chased a slippery avocado pit around the kitchen floor? Here's a simple way to remove the pit with a minimum of fuss. For the best flavor and texture, look for Hass-type avocados, which have pebbly dark skin. When an avocado is perfectly ripe, it should give to gentle fingertip pressure.

1. With a sharp, sturdy knife, cut the avocado in half symmetrically through its stem and flower ends, carefully cutting down all the way through the fruit to the pit.

2. Hold one side of the cut avocado securely in one hand. With your other hand, twist the other side to split the avocado in half. The pit will be embedded in one half.

3. Hold the half with the pit securely in one hand, while keeping your fingers safely clear of the cut surface and the pit. With the sharp edge of a sharp, sturdy knife, strike the pit firmly enough to embed the blade in it. (Or, if you prefer, scoop out the pit with a teaspoon or tablespoon.)

4. Twist the knife to dislodge the pit, which should lift out of the avocado half still stuck to the knife.

5. Carefully remove the pit from the blade and discard it.

6. If the avocado will not be used right away, rub the avocado's exposed surfaces with the cut side of a lemon half, or with some lemon juice, to prevent oxidation.

Pitting Olives

Many of my recipes call for pitted olives. Many upscale markets and good-quality gourmet delis now sell already-pitted olives of various kinds. And you can pit olives fairly easily with the help of an olive pitter, an inexpensive little kitchen gadget that grips an individual olive and, with the squeeze of your hand, pierces it and pushes out the pit. Or you can try this old-fashioned Mediterranean kitchen trick.

1. Spread the olives in a single layer on a clean kitchen towel or a double thickness of paper towels.

2. Fold the kitchen towel over the olives or, if you're using paper towels, place two sheets on top of the olives.

3. Using a rolling pin, press firmly down on the olives to crush them slightly, rolling across them as you do so.

4. Unfold the kitchen towel or remove the top paper towels. Sort through the olives, which will have split open to reveal their pits. Pick out and discard the pits. Repeat the process with any olives that have not yet split open.

Preparing Artichoke Hearts

The prickly exterior of artichokes betrays their membership in the thistle family. But beneath their protective armor hides a delicious, tender heart. Here's how to get to the heart of the matter with a minimum of fuss.

1. Artichoke hearts discolor quickly when exposed to air or when touched by carbon-steel knives. Use a clean, sharp stainless-steel knife and have a lemon handy to rub surfaces as soon as they are cut, thus preventing oxidation.

2. Starting at the broad base of the artichoke, break off the outer leaves, snapping them downward. Work round and round, gradually moving upward until only a cone of tightly packed inner leaves remains slightly more than halfway up the artichoke.

3. Slice off the top third or so of the artichoke to reveal the fibrous choke that's nestled inside the heart of the artichoke.

4. Using a small, sharp paring knife, peel off the dark green skin that remains around the base of the artichoke.

5. Using the knife or a small, sharp-edged spoon, dig into the center of the top of the artichoke to scoop out the fibrous choke, leaving the cup-shaped edible heart of the artichoke.

Shelling and Deveining Shrimp

*M*any dishes call for shrimp to be shelled before cooking. If you shell them, it's also necessary to devein them. The "vein" you're removing is actually the shrimp's gray-to-brownish-black digestive tract, which runs just below the surface along the outer curve of the shrimp.

1. To shell the shrimp, hold it with its legs toward you. Insert your thumbs between the two rows of legs and pull the shell apart and away. If you like, leave the tail fins on, or pull them off, too, if you prefer.

2. With the tip of a small, sharp knife, cut very shallowly along the shrimp's back to expose the vein. Pull out the vein with your fingertips or scrape it out with the tip of the knife.

A

Acqua Pazza with Sea Bass, Clams, and Mussels, 94–95

All-American Chicken Pot Pie, 118–120

All-American Potato Salad, 48–49

Almond Granita, 199–200

anchovy
   Pasta Puttanesca, 62

Angel Hair with Tomato Sauce, 64

appetizers, 3–21
   Black-and-Green-Olive Tapenade with Goat Cheese Crostini, 11
   California Guacamole, 4
   Chicken-and-Vegetable Quesadillas, 16–17
   Crab Cakes with Sweet Red Bell Pepper Sauce, 19–20
   Herbed Goat Cheese, 12
   Hot Spinach-Artichoke Dip, 14–15
   Potstickers with Pork and Dried Fruit Filling, 8–10
   Spicy Tomato-and-Basil Bruschetta, 13
   Tuna Tartare, 21
   wine suggestions, xix–xx
   Wolfgang's Vegetable Spring Rolls, 5–7

Yellow Finnish Potatoes with Crème Fraîche and Osetra Caviar, 18

apple
   Baked Apple Pouches with Cinnamon and Raisins, 178
   Braised Sweet-and-Sour Cabbage, 164
   Stir-Fried Wild Rice with Apples and Sun-Dried Cherries, 169
   Wolfgang's Tarte Tatin, 176–177

artichoke
   Calzone with Artichoke Hearts and Porcini Mushrooms, 57–58
   Chino Chopped-Vegetable Salad, 44–45
   hearts, preparing, 232
   Hot Spinach-Artichoke Dip, 14–15

Arugula, Goat Cheese Salad with Radicchio and, 38–39

asparagus
   Austrian White Asparagus with Browned Bread Crumbs, 158
   Stir-Fried Vegetables, 154–155

Austrian White Asparagus with Browned Bread Crumbs, 158

avocado
   California Guacamole, 4
   Chino Chopped-Vegetable Salad, 44–45
   pitting, 230

B

bacon
   Hearty Potato-and-Cheddar Soup with, 24–25
   Wolfgang's Bacon-Wrapped Meat Loaf, 126–127

Baked Apple Pouches with Cinnamon and Raisins, 178

Barbecued Butterflied Chicken with Orange-Sherry Marinade, 114–115

Basic Pasta Dough, 209–210

basil
   Angel Hair with Tomato Sauce, 64
   Basil-Garlic Vinaigrette, 227
   Basil Oil, 224
   My Favorite Tomato Sauce, 63
   My Mother's Garden Vegetable Soup, 27

basil (*cont.*)

Pasta Puttanesca, 62

Spicy Tomato-and-Basil Bruschetta, 13

Zucchini with Basil and Tomatoes, 157

beef

Beef Stew with Winter Vegetables and Red Wine, 132–133

Classic Beef Lasagne, 67–68

Hearty Beef Bolognese, 65–66

My Beef Goulash, 134–135

New York Steaks with Four Peppercorns and Port Wine Sauce, 130–131

Roasted Beef Tenderloin with Smoky Tomato-Chili Salsa, 136–137

Spicy Asian Beef Burgers with Shiitake Mushrooms, 128–129

wine suggestions, xxii

Wolfgang's Bacon-Wrapped Meat Loaf, 126–127

bell peppers

Acqua Pazza with Sea Bass, Clams, and Mussels, 94–95

Crab Cakes with Sweet Red Bell Pepper Sauce, 19–20

My Mother's Chicken-Stuffed Bell Peppers with Tomato Sauce, 116–117

Pan-Roasted Chicken Breasts Stuffed with Bell Peppers with Sweet Green Onion Sauce, 106–107

Roasted Tomato and Pepper Salsa, 16–17

Stir-Fried Vegetables, 154–155

Wolfgang's Vegetable Spring Rolls, 5–7

Biscuits, Buttermilk, with Parmesan and Onion, 170–171

Black-and-Green-Olive Tapenade with Goat Cheese Crostini, 11

Black Bass, Roasted, on Jasmine Rice with Miso Glaze, 101

Black Bean Sauce, Lobster Imperial in, 90–91

bok choy

Lobster Imperial in Black Bean Sauce, 90–91

Stir-Fried Vegetables, 154–155

Bouquet Garni, 223

Braised Chestnuts, 167–168

Braised Sweet-and-Sour Cabbage, 164

bread

Black-and-Green-Olive Tapenade with Goat Cheese Crostini, 11

Buttermilk Biscuits with Parmesan and Onion, 170–171

Focaccia, 172–173

Spicy Tomato-and-Basil Bruschetta, 13

See also pizza

broccoli

Stir-Fried Vegetables, 154–155

Brown Chicken Stock, 205

Brown Veal Stock, 207

Bruschetta, Spicy Tomato-and-Basil, 13

Bucatini with Mussels, Clams, and Oven-Dried Tomatoes, 71–72

burgers

Spicy Asian Beef, with Shiitake Mushrooms, 128–129

Turkey Mushroom, with Chunky Tomato Salsa Compote, 122–123

Buttermilk Biscuits with Parmesan and Onion, 170–171

butternut squash

Beef Stew with Winter Vegetables and Red Wine, 132–133

c

cabbage

Braised Sweet-and-Sour, 164

Chinois Chicken Salad, 42–43

Wolfgang's Vegetable Spring Rolls, 5–7

cake

Decadent Warm Chocolate Cupcakes with Molten Centers, 179–180

My Favorite Chocolate Cake, 181–182

California Guacamole, 4

Calzone with Artichoke Hearts and Porcini Mushrooms, 57–58

Cannellini Beans, Pan-Seared Sea Bass with Braised Escarole, Cherry Tomato Vinaigrette and, 96–98

capers/caper berries

Insalata Pantesca, 46

Pasta Puttanesca, 62

Sea Bass with Lemon and Caper Sauce, 99–100

Caramelized Lemon-Lime Tart, 187–188

carrot

Chino Farm Carrot-and-Ginger Soup, 26

Catalonian Fire-Roasted Rack of Lamb, 147–149

caviar

Pizza with Smoked Salmon and, 54

Yellow Finnish Potatoes with Crème Fraîche and Osetra, 18

cheese
  All-American Chicken Pot Pie, 118–120
  Black-and-Green-Olive Tapenade with Goat Cheese Crostini, 11
  Buttermilk Biscuits with Parmesan and Onion, 170–171
  Calzone with Artichoke Hearts and Porcini Mushrooms, 57–58
  Chicken-and-Vegetable Quesadillas, 16–17
  Classic Beef Lasagne, 67–68
  Classic French Onion Soup, 34–35
  Fettuccine Wolf-fredo with Grilled Chicken, 59–61
  Four Seasons Pizza, 55–56
  Goat Cheese Salad with Arugula and Radicchio, 38–39
  Hearty Potato-and-Cheddar Soup with Bacon, 24–25
  Herbed Goat, 12
  Hot Spinach-Artichoke Dip, 14–15
  Potato Galette with Goat, 163
  Spicy Chicken Pizza, 52–53
  White Corn Agnolotti, 75–77
cheesecake
  Classic Spago, 192–193
  Cookies-and-Cream, 189–191
Cherries, Stir-Fried Wild Rice with Apples and Sun-Dried, 169
Cherry Tomato Vinaigrette, 97–98
Chestnuts, Braised, 167–168
chicken. *See* poultry
Chicken-and-Vegetable Quesadillas, 16–17
Chicken Pot Pie Soup, 28–29
Chicken Stock, 204
chiffonade, 229

Chili and Garlic Oil, 225
chili peppers
  California Guacamole, 4
  Catalonian Fire-Roasted Rack of Lamb, 147–149
  Jalapeño Cream, 32–33
  Roasted Beef Tenderloin with Smoky Tomato-Chili Salsa, 136–137
  Roasted Tomato and Pepper Salsa, 16–17
  Spicy Asian Beef Burgers with Shiitake Mushrooms, 128–129
  Spicy Chicken Pizza, 52–53
  Spicy Shrimp Tempura with Cilantro, 82–83
  Tortilla Soup, 30–31
Chinese Hot Mustard Sauce, 5
Chinese Mustard Vinaigrette, 42–43
Chino Chopped-Vegetable Salad, 44–45
Chino Farm Carrot-and-Ginger Soup, 26
Chinois Chicken Salad, 42–43
Chinois Grilled Lamb Chops with Cilantro-Mint Vinaigrette, 150–151
chocolate
  Chocolate Shortbread Footballs, 183–184
  Cookies-and-Cream Cheesecake, 189–191
  Decadent Warm Chocolate Cupcakes with Molten Centers, 179–180
  My Favorite Chocolate Cake, 181–182
  White Chocolate Malt Ice Cream, 198
Chunky Tomato Salsa Compote, 122–123

cilantro
  California Guacamole, 4
  Cilantro-Mint Vinaigrette, 150–151
  Spicy Shrimp Tempura with, 82–83
  Wolfgang's Vegetable Spring Rolls, 5–7
clams
  Acqua Pazza with Sea Bass, Clams, and Mussels, 94–95
  Bucatini with Mussels, Clams, and Oven-Dried Tomatoes, 71–72
  Corn Chowder with Littleneck Clams and Jalapeño Cream, 32–33
  Four Seasons Pizza, 55–56
Classic Beef Lasagne, 67–68
Classic French Onion Soup, 34–35
Classic Spago Cheesecake, 192–193
cookies
  Chocolate Shortbread Footballs, 183–184
  Cookies-and-Cream Cheesecake, 189–191
corn
  Chino Chopped-Vegetable Salad, 44–45
  Corn Chowder with Littleneck Clams and Jalapeño Cream, 32–33
  Tortilla Soup, 30–31
  White Corn Agnolotti, 75–77
Court Bouillon, 208
Crab Cakes with Sweet Red Bell Pepper Sauce, 19–20
cream
  Dill, 226
  Jalapeño, 32–33

Creamy Mashed Potatoes with
    Caramelized Onions, 160–161
Crispy Shrimp with Chinese
    Noodles and Spicy Garlic
    Sauce, 84–85
Crostini, Black-and-Green-Olive
    Tapenade with Goat Cheese,
    11
cucumber
    Spago Cucumber Salad, 47

D

Decadent Warm Chocolate
    Cupcakes with Molten
    Centers, 179–180
dessert
    Almond Granita, 199–200
    Baked Apple Pouches with
        Cinnamon and Raisins, 178
    Caramelized Lemon-Lime Tart,
        187–188
    Chocolate Shortbread Footballs,
        183–184
    Classic Spago Cheesecake,
        192–193
    Cookies-and-Cream Cheese-
        cake, 189–191
    Decadent Warm Chocolate
        Cupcakes with Molten
        Centers, 179–180
    Kaiserschmarren, 194–195
    Melon Granita, 201
    My Favorite Chocolate Cake,
        181–182
    Raspberries in Puff Pastry,
        185–186
    Salzburger Nockerln with Fresh
        Raspberry Jam, 196–197
    White Chocolate Malt Ice
        Cream, 198
    wine suggestions, xxii
    Wolfgang's Tarte Tatin, 176–177

Dijon Mustard Vinaigrette, 44–45
Dill Cream, 226
Dipping Sauce, 9–10
dips and spreads
    Black-and-Green-Olive
        Tapenade with Goat Cheese
        Crostini, 11
    California Guacamole, 4
    Herbed Goat Cheese, 12
    Hot Spinach-Artichoke Dip,
        14–15
    Roasted Tomato and Pepper
        Salsa, 16–17
Double-Blanched Garlic, 220
Dry-Fried String Beans, 156
dumplings
    Chicken Pot Pie Soup, 28–29
    Potstickers with Pork and Dried
        Fruit Filling, 8–10
    Spaetzle, 165–166

E

eggplant
    Acqua Pazza with Sea Bass,
        Clams, and Mussels, 94–95
    Stir-Fried Vegetables, 154–155
escarole
    Pan-Seared Sea Bass with
        Cannellini Beans, Braised
        Escarole, and Cherry Tomato
        Vinaigrette, 96–98

F

Fettuccine Wolf-fredo with Grilled
    Chicken, 59–61
Fish Stock, 206
Focaccia, 172–173
Four Seasons Pizza, 55–56
French Onion Soup, Classic, 34–35
Fresh Sweet Italian Fennel Sausage,
    145–146
Fried Spinach Leaves, 159

G

garlic
    Basil-Garlic Vinaigrette, 227
    Chili and Garlic Oil, 225
    Double-Blanched, 220
    Grilled Chicken Breasts with
        Garlic and Parsley, 108–109
    Roasted-Garlic Mashed
        Potatoes, 162
    Roasted Whole, 219
ginger
    Chino Farm Carrot-and-Ginger
        Soup, 26
    Grilled Shrimp with Ginger and
        Lime, 86
    Lobster with Sweet, 87–88
glass noodles
    Wolfgang's Vegetable Spring
        Rolls, 5–7
Goat Cheese Salad with Arugula
    and Radicchio, 38–39
granita
    Almond, 199–200
    Melon, 201
Greek Salad Dressing, 228
Greek Shrimp Salad, 40–41
green beans/haricots verts
    Chino Chopped-Vegetable
        Salad, 44–45
    Crispy Shrimp with Chinese
        Noodles and Spicy Garlic
        Sauce, 84–85
    Dry-Fried String Beans, 156
    Grilled Chicken Breasts with Garlic
        and Parsley, 108–109
    Grilled Chicken Kebabs with
        Lemon and Thyme, 112–113
    Grilled Italian Chicken with
        Summer Squash, 110–111
    Grilled Shrimp with Ginger and
        Lime, 86
Guacamole, California, 4

H

Hearty Beef Bolognese, 65–66

Hearty Potato-and-Cheddar Soup
with Bacon, 24–25

Herbed Goat Cheese, 12

Hot Spinach-Artichoke Dip,
14–15

I

Ice Cream, White Chocolate Malt,
198

Insalata Pantesca, 46

J

jalapeño peppers. *See* chili peppers

julienne, 229

K

Kaiserschmarren, 194–195

L

lamb

Catalonian Fire-Roasted Rack of
Lamb, 147–149

Chinois Grilled Lamb Chops
with Cilantro-Mint Vinaigrette,
150–151

wine suggestions, xxii

Lasagne, Classic Beef, 67–68

lemon

Caramelized Lemon-Lime Tart,
187–188

Grilled Chicken Kebabs with
Lemon and Thyme,
112–113

Sea Bass with Lemon and Caper
Sauce, 99–100

lime

Caramelized Lemon-Lime Tart,
187–188

Grilled Shrimp with Ginger and,
86

lobster

Lobster Imperial in Black Bean
Sauce, 90–91

with Sweet Ginger, 87–88

M

Marinated and Glazed Swordfish,
102–103

meat. *See* bacon; beef; lamb; pork;
veal

Meatballs, My Special Spaghetti
and, 69–70

Meat Loaf, Wolfgang's Bacon-
Wrapped, 126–127

Melon Granita, 201

Minced Veal or Pork with
Chanterelles, Paprika Cream
Sauce, and Noodles, 141–142

mushroom

Calzone with Artichoke Hearts
and Porcini, 57–58

Chicken Pot Pie Soup, 28–29

Four Seasons Pizza, 55–56

Minced Veal or Pork with
Chanterelles, Paprika Cream
Sauce, and Noodles, 141–
142

My Mother's Chicken-Stuffed
Bell Peppers with Tomato
Sauce, 116–117

Spicy Asian Beef Burgers with
Shiitake, 128–129

Stir-Fried Vegetables, 154–155

Turkey Mushroom Burgers with
Chunky Tomato Salsa
Compote, 122–123

Wild Mushroom Risotto,
78–79

Wolfgang's Bacon-Wrapped
Meat Loaf, 126–127

Wolfgang's Vegetable Spring
Rolls, 5–7

mussels

Acqua Pazza with Sea Bass,
Clams, and Mussels, 94–95

Bucatini with Mussels, Clams,
and Oven-Dried Tomatoes,
71–72

mustard

Chinese Hot Mustard Sauce, 5

Chinese Mustard Vinaigrette,
42–43

Dijon Mustard Vinaigrette,
44–45

Mustard Vinaigrette, 38–39

My Beef Goulash, 134–135

My Favorite Chocolate Cake,
181–182

My Favorite Tomato Sauce, 63

My Mother's Chicken-Stuffed Bell
Peppers with Tomato Sauce,
116–117

My Mother's Garden Vegetable
Soup, 27

My Special Spaghetti and
Meatballs, 69–70

N

New York Steaks with Four
Peppercorns and Port Wine
Sauce, 130–131

nuts, toasting, 221

O

oil

Basil, 224

Chili and Garlic, 225

olives

Black-and-Green-Olive
Tapenade with Goat Cheese
Crostini, 11

Insalata Pantesca, 46

Pasta Puttanesca, 62

pitting, 231

onion
>   Buttermilk Biscuits with Parmesan and Onion, 170–171
>   Chicken Pot Pie Soup, 28–29
>   Classic French Onion Soup, 34–35
>   Creamy Mashed Potatoes with Caramelized, 160–161
>   Pan-Roasted Chicken Breasts Stuffed with Bell Peppers with Sweet Green Onion Sauce, 106–107
>   Rack of Pork with Caramelized Maple Onions, 143–144
Orange-Sherry Marinade, 114–115
Oven-Dried Tomatoes, 218

P

Pan-Roasted Chicken Breasts Stuffed with Bell Peppers with Sweet Green Onion Sauce, 106–107
Pan-Seared Sea Bass with Cannellini Beans, Braised Escarole, and Cherry Tomato Vinaigrette, 96–98
Parmesan Cream Sauce, 59–61
parsley
>   Grilled Chicken Breasts with Garlic and, 108–109
parsnips
>   Beef Stew with Winter Vegetables and Red Wine, 132–133
pasta, 59–79
>   Angel Hair with Tomato Sauce, 64
>   Basic Pasta Dough, 209–210
>   Bucatini with Mussels, Clams, and Oven-Dried Tomatoes, 71–72
>   Classic Beef Lasagne, 67–68

Crispy Shrimp with Chinese Noodles and Spicy Garlic Sauce, 84–85
Fettuccine Wolf-fredo with Grilled Chicken, 59–61
Hearty Beef Bolognese, 65–66
Minced Veal or Pork with Chanterelles, Paprika Cream Sauce, and Noodles, 141–142
My Favorite Tomato Sauce, 63
My Special Spaghetti and Meatballs, 69–70
Pasta Puttanesca, 62
Pumpkin Ravioli, 73–74
White Corn Agnolotti, 75–77
wine suggestions, xx
peppercorns
>   New York Steaks with Four Peppercorns and Port Wine Sauce, 130–131
>   Seared Tuna au Poivre, 92–93
peppers. See bell peppers; chili peppers
Pistou, 27
pizza, 52–58
>   Calzone with Artichoke Hearts and Porcini Mushrooms, 57–58
>   Four Seasons, 55–56
>   Pizza Dough, 211–212
>   with Smoked Salmon and Caviar, 54
>   Spicy Chicken, 52–53
>   wine suggestions, xx
pork
>   Fresh Sweet Italian Fennel Sausage, 145–146
>   Minced Veal or Pork with Chanterelles, Paprika Cream Sauce, and Noodles, 141–142
>   Potstickers with Pork and Dried Fruit Filling, 8–10

Rack of Pork with Caramelized Maple Onions, 143–144
wine suggestions, xxi–xxii
Wolfgang's Bacon-Wrapped Meat Loaf, 126–127
See also bacon
potato
>   All-American Potato Salad, 48–49s
>   Creamy Mashed Potatoes with Caramelized Onions, 160–161
>   Hearty Potato-and-Cheddar Soup with Bacon, 24–25
>   Insalata Pantesca, 46
>   Potato Galette with Goat Cheese, 163
>   Roasted-Garlic Mashed Potatoes, 162
>   Wiener Schnitzel with Warm Potato Salad, 138–140
>   Yellow Finnish Potatoes with Crème Fraîche and Osetra Caviar, 18
Pot Pie, All-American Chicken, 118–120
Potstickers with Pork and Dried Fruit Filling, 8–10
poultry, 105–123
>   All-American Chicken Pot Pie, 118–120
>   Barbecued Butterflied Chicken with Orange-Sherry Marinade, 114–115
>   Brown Chicken Stock, 205
>   Chicken-and-Vegetable Quesadillas, 16–17
>   Chicken Pot Pie Soup, 28–29
>   Chicken Stock, 204
>   Chinois Chicken Salad, 42–43
>   Fettuccine Wolf-fredo with Grilled Chicken, 59–61

Grilled Chicken Breasts with
Garlic and Parsley, 108–109
Grilled Chicken Kebabs with
Lemon and Thyme, 112–113
Grilled Italian Chicken with
Summer Squash, 110–111
My Mother's Chicken-Stuffed
Bell Peppers with Tomato
Sauce, 116–117
Pan-Roasted Chicken Breasts
Stuffed with Bell Peppers with
Sweet Green Onion Sauce,
106–107
Spicy Chicken Pizza, 52–53
Turkey Mushroom Burgers
with Chunky Tomato Salsa
Compote, 122–123
Wiener Backhendl, 121
wine suggestions, xxi
prosciutto
Four Seasons Pizza, 55–56
Puff Pastry, 213–215
Raspberries in, 185–186
Wolfgang's Tarte Tatin,
176–177
Pumpkin Ravioli, 73–74

Q

Quesadillas, Chicken-and-
Vegetable, 16–17

R

Rack of Pork with Caramelized
Maple Onions, 143–144
radicchio
Chino Chopped-Vegetable
Salad, 44–45
Goat Cheese Salad with Arugula
and Radicchio, 38–39
raspberry
Raspberries in Puff Pastry,
185–186

Salzburger Nockerln with Fresh
Raspberry Jam, 196–197
rice
Roasted Black Bass on Jasmine
Rice with Miso Glaze, 101
Stir-Fried Wild Rice with
Apples and Sun-Dried
Cherries, 169
Wild Mushroom Risotto, 78–79
Risotto, Wild Mushroom, 78–79
Roasted Beef Tenderloin with
Smoky Tomato-Chili Salsa,
136–137
Roasted Black Bass on Jasmine
Rice with Miso Glaze, 101
Roasted-Garlic Mashed Potatoes,
162
Roasted Tomato and Pepper Salsa,
16–17
Roasted Whole Garlic, 219
Romesco Sauce, 147–149

S

salad, 37–49
All-American Potato, 48–49
Chino Chopped-Vegetable,
44–45
Chinois Chicken, 42–43
Goat Cheese, with Arugula and
Radicchio, 38–39
Greek Shrimp, 40–41
Insalata Pantesca, 46
Spago Cucumber, 47
Wiener Schnitzel with Warm
Potato, 138–140
wine suggestions, xx
salad dressings
Basil-Garlic Vinaigrette, 227
Chinese Mustard Vinaigrette,
42–43
Dijon Mustard Vinaigrette,
44–45

Greek Salad Dressing, 228
Mustard Vinaigrette, 38–39
salmon
Pizza with Smoked Salmon and
Caviar, 54
salsa
Chunky Tomato Salsa Compote,
122–123
Roasted Tomato and Pepper,
16–17
Tomato-Chili, 136–137
Salzburger Nockerln with Fresh
Raspberry Jam, 196–197
sauce
Chinese Hot Mustard, 5
Chunky Tomato Salsa Compote,
122–123
Dipping, 9–10
My Favorite Tomato, 63
Parmesan Cream, 59–61
Roasted Tomato and Pepper
Salsa, 16–17
Romesco, 147–149
Strawberry, 194–195
Sweet Red Bell Pepper,
19–20
Tomato-Chili Salsa, 136–
137
Sausage, Fresh Sweet Italian
Fennel, 145–146
sea bass
Acqua Pazza with Sea Bass,
Clams, and Mussels, 94–95
with Lemon and Caper Sauce,
99–100
Pan-Seared Sea Bass with
Cannellini Beans, Braised
Escarole, and Cherry Tomato
Vinaigrette, 96–98
seafood, 81–103
Acqua Pazza with Sea Bass,
Clams, and Mussels, 94–95

seafood (*cont.*)

Bucatini with Mussels, Clams, and Oven-Dried Tomatoes, 71–72

Corn Chowder with Littleneck Clams and Jalapeño Cream, 32–33

Crab Cakes with Sweet Red Bell Pepper Sauce, 19–20

Crispy Shrimp with Chinese Noodles and Spicy Garlic Sauce, 84–85

Fish Stock, 206

Four Seasons Pizza, 55–56

Greek Shrimp Salad, 40–41

Grilled Shrimp with Ginger and Lime, 86

Lobster Imperial in Black Bean Sauce, 90–91

Lobster with Sweet Ginger, 87–88

Marinated and Glazed Swordfish, 102–103

Pan-Seared Sea Bass with Cannellini Beans, Braised Escarole, and Cherry Tomato Vinaigrette, 96–98

Pizza with Smoked Salmon and Caviar, 54

Roasted Black Bass on Jasmine Rice with Miso Glaze, 101

Sea Bass with Lemon and Caper Sauce, 99–100

Seared Tuna au Poivre, 92–93

Spicy Shrimp Tempura with Cilantro, 82–83

Tuna Tartare, 21

wine suggestions, xx–xxi

Yellow Finnish Potatoes with Crème Fraîche and Osetra Caviar, 18

Seared Tuna au Poivre, 92–93

shrimp

Crispy Shrimp with Chinese Noodles and Spicy Garlic Sauce, 84–85

Greek Shrimp Salad, 40–41

Grilled Shrimp with Ginger and Lime, 86

shelling and deveining, 233

Spicy Shrimp Tempura with Cilantro, 82–83

snow peas

Stir-Fried Vegetables, 154–55

soup, 23–35

Chicken Pot Pie, 28–29

Chino Farm Carrot-and-Ginger, 26

Classic French Onion, 34–35

Corn Chowder with Littleneck Clams and Jalapeño Cream, 32–33

Hearty Potato-and-Cheddar Soup with Bacon, 24–25

My Mother's Garden Vegetable, 27

Tortilla, 30–31

wine suggestions, xix–xx

Spaetzle, 165–166

Spago Cucumber Salad, 47

spices, toasting and grinding whole, 222

Spicy Asian Beef Burgers with Shiitake Mushrooms, 128–129

Spicy Chicken Pizza, 52–53

Spicy Shrimp Tempura with Cilantro, 82–83

Spicy Tomato-and-Basil Bruschetta, 13

spinach

Fried Spinach Leaves, 159

Hot Spinach-Artichoke Dip, 14–15

spreads. *See* dips and spreads

Spring Rolls, Wolfgang's Vegetable, 5–7

stew

Beef Stew with Winter Vegetables and Red Wine, 132–133

My Beef Goulash, 134–135

Stir-Fried Vegetables, 154–155

Stir-Fried Wild Rice with Apples and Sun-Dried Cherries, 169

stock

Brown Chicken, 205

Brown Veal, 207

Chicken, 204

Court Bouillon, 208

Fish, 206

Strawberry Sauce, 194–195

Sugar Dough, 216

Summer Squash, Grilled Italian Chicken with, 110–111

Sweet Red Bell Pepper Sauce, 19–20

Swordfish, Marinated and Glazed, 102–103

T

Tapenade, Black-and-Green-Olive, with Goat Cheese Crostini, 11

Tarte Tatin, Wolfgang's, 176–177

Tempura, Spicy Shrimp, with Cilantro, 82–83

tomato

Acqua Pazza with Sea Bass, Clams, and Mussels, 94–95

Angel Hair with Tomato Sauce, 64

Beef Stew with Winter Vegetables and Red Wine, 132–133

Black-and-Green-Olive Tapenade with Goat Cheese Crostini, 11

Bucatini with Mussels, Clams, and Oven-Dried Tomatoes, 71–72

Catalonian Fire-Roasted Rack of Lamb, 147–149

Chino Chopped-Vegetable Salad, 44–45

Four Seasons Pizza, 55–56

Hearty Beef Bolognese, 65–66

Insalata Pantesca, 46

My Favorite Tomato Sauce, 63

My Mother's Chicken-Stuffed Bell Peppers with Tomato Sauce, 116–117

My Mother's Garden Vegetable Soup, 27

My Special Spaghetti and Meatballs, 69–70

oven-dried, 218

Pan-Seared Sea Bass with Cannellini Beans, Braised Escarole, and Cherry Tomato Vinaigrette, 96–98

Pasta Puttanesca, 62

peeled and seeded, 217

Roasted Beef Tenderloin with Smoky Tomato-Chili Salsa, 136–137

Roasted Tomato and Pepper Salsa, 16–17

Spicy Chicken Pizza, 52–53

Spicy Tomato-and-Basil Bruschetta, 13

Tomato-Chili Salsa, 136–137

Tomato Concassé, 217

Tortilla Soup, 30–31

Turkey Mushroom Burgers with Chunky Tomato Salsa Compote, 122–123

Zucchini with Basil and, 157

tortillas
  Chicken-and-Vegetable Quesadillas, 16–17
  Tortilla Soup, 30–31

tuna
  Seared Tuna au Poivre, 92–93
  Tuna Tartare, 21

turkey. See poultry

Turkey Mushroom Burgers with Chunky Tomato Salsa Compote, 122–123

V

veal
  Brown Veal Stock, 207
  Minced Veal or Pork with Chanterelles, Paprika Cream Sauce, and Noodles, 141–142
  My Special Spaghetti and Meatballs, 69–70
  Wiener Schnitzel with Warm Potato Salad, 138–140
  wine suggestions, xxi–xxii
  Wolfgang's Bacon-Wrapped Meat Loaf, 126–127

vinaigrette
  Basil-Garlic, 227
  Cherry Tomato, 97–98
  Chinese Mustard, 42–43
  Cilantro-Mint, 150–151
  Dijon Mustard, 44–45
  Mustard, 38–39

W

White Chocolate Malt Ice Cream, 198

White Corn Agnolotti, 75–77

Wiener Backhendl, 121

Wiener Schnitzel with Warm Potato Salad, 138–140

Wild Mushroom Risotto, 78–79

wine
  Beef Stew with Winter Vegetables and Red Wine, 132–133
  Bucatini with Mussels, Clams, and Oven-Dried Tomatoes, 71–72
  Lobster with Sweet Ginger, 87–88
  New York Steaks with Four Peppercorns and Port Wine Sauce, 130–131
  suggestions for serving, xix–xxii

Wolfgang's Bacon-Wrapped Meat Loaf, 126–127

Wolfgang's Tarte Tatin, 176–177

Wolfgang's Vegetable Spring Rolls, 5–7

Y

Yellow Finnish Potatoes with Crème Fraîche and Osetra Caviar, 18

Z

zucchini
  Acqua Pazza with Sea Bass, Clams, and Mussels, 94–95
  with Basil and Tomatoes, 157
  Grilled Italian Chicken with Summer Squash, 110–111

WOLFGANG PUCK began his formal chef's training in his native Austria at the age of fourteen. His classical training as a French chef continued in the kitchens of the Hôtel de Paris in Monaco, Maxim's in Paris, and L'Oustau de Baumanière in Provence. Shortly after his arrival in Los Angeles in 1975, he drew crowds to Ma Maison, where he was chef and part owner.

In 1982, Puck, along with his wife and business partner, Barbara Lazaroff, opened the first Spago restaurant on the Sunset Strip, which earned enduring accolades for its informal yet sophisticated cuisine. In the years since, they have opened Chinois on Main in Santa Monica; Spago branches in Beverly Hills, Palo Alto, Las Vegas, Chicago, and Maui; Postrio in San Francisco and Las Vegas; Granita in Malibu; Trattoria del Lupo in Las Vegas; and Vert brasserie in Hollywood's new Hollywood & Highland center—home to the Oscars, for which Puck cooks for the annual Governor's Ball from his new on-site catering kitchen.

Puck has also opened seventeen Wolfgang Puck Cafe casual-dining restaurants and many quick-casual Wolfgang Puck Expresses.

Wolfgang Puck is the star of his own Emmy Award–winning television show on the Food Network, and appears regularly on ABC's *Good Morning America*. He is the author of *Wolfgang Puck's Pizza, Pasta, and More!, Adventures in the Kitchen, The Wolfgang Puck Cookbook,* and *Wolfgang Puck's Modern French Cooking for the American Kitchen.* The winner of three James Beard awards, among numerous other honors, he is one of the most renowned chefs of our time. Puck and his wife, Barbara Lazaroff, live in Los Angeles with their two sons.